Praise for *Moral*

"As bitcoin gains widespread adoption, many seek to understand its significance beyond economic hype. In *Moral Money*, Eric Sammons explains how the type of money we use has profound moral implications, examining bitcoin through both economic and moral principles to show how it stands apart from debased fiat currencies and the wild west of other cryptocurrencies as a morally sound alternative for the future. Drawing from Scripture and Tradition, Sammons's accessible yet thorough introduction to bitcoin offers readers a deeper framework for understanding money and demonstrates why the money we choose matters as much as how we choose to use it."

— ***Michael Goldstein,*** aka "Bitstein," Founder
and President, Satoshi Nakamoto Institute

"Bitcoin can be obscure and even scary to many people. And money, despite its vital role in commerce, has always been a morally complex topic — especially in an age when the government degrades its value as a matter of policy. Into this shadowy thicket, Eric Sammons shines a bright light. He illuminates both the function and nature of money and makes a persuasive case that bitcoin is both morally and financially superior to the currencies controlled by all modern states. Let's hope this book provokes a serious debate among serious Christians. Our future well-being may depend on it."

— ***Jay W. Richards,*** Author, *Money, Greed, and
God: The Christian Case for Free Enterprise*

"In *Moral Money*, the always-clear-thinking Sammons delivers a compelling moral case for bitcoin that transcends our typical rote financial discourse. Examining money through a moral lens, he articulates how our current fiat system systematically undermines human flourishing while eroding purchasing power, favoring the elite over the poor, and incentivizing shortsighted consumption patterns. Money itself is not a typical topic of discussion among Christians, but Christians should be the first to understand and appreciate the ill effects of immoral money. Unfortunately, we've been late to the game. That is changing with Sammons's important primer on 'the most moral form of money in human history.'"

— ***Andrew Flattery, CFP®,*** Principal, Flattery Wealth Management

"Bitcoin can be overwhelming, but Eric Sammons's charity for the reader shines through with relatable metaphors and clear explanations. Sammons goes beyond describing how bitcoin works: he presents a cohesive view of its place in monetary history, Christian teachings, and the modern fiat world. Along the way, there's an honest recognition that bitcoin is imperfect but has value despite its limitations. I encourage those who reject all of 'crypto' to jump to the chapter on objections and those who embrace all of 'crypto' to skip to the chapter on other cryptocurrencies. Written by a real bitcoiner and complete with practical advice, *Moral Money* is a book you can confidently share with friends, family, and clergy."

— ***Pierre Rochard,*** Cofounder, Satoshi Nakamoto Institute

"Bitcoin is a revolutionary invention that is changing the world for the better, yet so few people understand it, let alone use it. That's a shame because, as Eric Sammons lucidly explains in *Moral Money*, bitcoin's properties make it the best sound money that the world has ever seen, providing a way to end the injustice and evil rampant in our centrally controlled, fiat-currency monetary systems."

— ***Devin Rose,*** Author, *The Fiefdom Chronicles* series and *Lionheart Catholic*

"In an age where governments finance unjust wars through the unchecked printing of fiat currency, an alternative system is needed to bring peace. In *Moral Money*, Eric Sammons demonstrates why bitcoin is that alternative due to its decentralized nature and built-in features that make state manipulation impossible. If we truly seek to stop the seemingly never-ending conflicts that plague our world, we must strike at the root cause: our corrupt monetary system. This book is a must-read for anyone who values peace, sound money, and a more stable future for generations to come. It also serves as an excellent primer for those seeking an understanding of what bitcoin is."

— ***Dave DeCamp,*** News Editor, Antiwar.com

Moral Money

Moral Money

ERIC SAMMONS

MORAL MONEY

The Case for Bitcoin

SOPHIA INSTITUTE PRESS
Manchester, New Hampshire

Sophia Institute Press
Box 5284, Manchester, NH 03108
1-800-888-9344
www.SophiaInstitute.com

Sophia Institute Press® is a registered trademark of Sophia Institute.

paperback ISBN 979-8-88911-548-9

ebook ISBN 979-8-88911-549-6

Library of Congress Control Number: 2025936442

First printing

Dedication

To my Free-Market Economics homeschool class:
Helping you think got me thinking.

Contents

Preface

WHEN I FIRST got involved with the bitcoin community in 2013, I felt like a fish out of water. Here I was, a middle-aged, middle-class, socially conservative practicing Catholic, surrounded by mostly young, socially liberal libertarian/anarchist agnostics and atheists. Our worldviews were at odds and our personal moral codes were definitely not aligned. Whenever I entered an online bitcoin forum, I knew I had little in common with the other participants, other than bitcoin. I might not have been the only Catholic involved with bitcoin at the time, but it surely felt like it. Yet I persevered because I was convinced that this technological and economic marvel known as bitcoin could change the world for the better.

A funny thing has happened over the years. I've seen the bitcoin community transform from an eclectic group of anti-government libertarians who advocated the buying and selling of illegal drugs and the overthrow of the government to a community that emphasizes personal fiscal responsibility and eschews instant gratification. Listening to a bitcoin podcast recently, I heard the host mention a fellow bitcoiner who was "pregnant again," and the host partly credited the mom's decision to have another child to the couple's financial stability due to bitcoin. The guests of the show—all die-hard bitcoiners—were ecstatic about the good news and told similar stories from their own lives. A 2024 documentary called *God Bless Bitcoin* emphasized how bitcoin conformed to the moral teachings of the world's major religions, and it too mentioned that people were having more babies due to their financial situation being secured by bitcoin.

Watching this transformation over the past eleven years has been remarkable, and I've realized it's no coincidence. Bitcoin itself is driving it, because bitcoin rewards long-term thinking, fiscal responsibility, and honest dealings. Yes, bitcoin is still used — and always will be used — by criminals and other immoral actors, just like the dollar. Unlike the dollar, however, the design of bitcoin can lead people to better lives, while our current monetary system incentivizes excessive consumption and rewards the corrupt powerful elites of this world. In this book I'll explain why this is and why all people of good will should embrace the bitcoin revolution, not just because it can improve the world's economics, but also because it can improve individuals' moral choices.

Moral Money

Introduction

He who loves money will not
be satisfied with money.

—Ecclesiastes 5:10

HAVE YOU NOTICED that something's wrong with our money?

Oh, you might not think of it that way, but I bet you've noticed. Perhaps you've wondered why prices at the grocery store keep going up ... and up and up. Or why your 26-year-old son can't afford a modest house, even though he makes far more than you did when you bought your first home. Or why everyone needs to be an investment expert just to stay afloat financially. You might blame this politician or that policy decision, but no matter who's in charge and no matter what they do, these problems persist.

Any way you slice it, something's wrong. In this book, I make the argument that the misgivings you have about our money system, whether latent or overt, are correct. Our money, in fact, is *immoral*. But this book isn't just about what's wrong with our money; it argues for a new form of money, the most moral that's ever been used: bitcoin.

Now, today people get uncomfortable with talk of morality. "Don't push your morality on me!" Bring up the idea of "morality" at a party and wait for the jokes about the old "Church Lady" skit from *Saturday Night Live*—Dana Carvey scolding his guests and blaming their bad behavior on Satan (if I'm dating myself here, look it up on YouTube). "Morality? How quaint!" says modern man. Yet nearly everyone lives by some system of morality, and most people share a lot of the same ideas about basic right and wrong.

If you hear your friend was mugged and had his wallet stolen, your initial reaction will likely be anger at the injustice of what happened. You know instinctively that the robbery was wrong; i.e., it was *immoral* on the mugger's part to steal from your friend. It doesn't matter if you are Christian or Jewish or an agnostic or an atheist—you just *know* what happened was wrong. So when I talk about the morality of money in this book, I'm tapping into that instinct of right and wrong we all share, what philosophers call the "natural law."

So, what does money have to do with morality?

Quite a lot, actually.

Morality consists of the choices we make, both good and bad. By "good" and "bad" I don't mean simply whether or not the choice was helpful or was a mistake; I mean whether it was *right* or *wrong*, based on that natural law we all instinctively accept. Moral choices are considered right and immoral choices are wrong. Some choices are neutral, of course, such as whether to have chocolate or vanilla ice cream, but many of the choices we make each day are choices steeped in morality.

And morality doesn't just include our individual choices; even *systems* can be moral or immoral. Slavery is an immoral system, one that institutionalizes immoral choices made by many individuals. The network of hospitals set up in the Middle Ages was a moral system, as it gave people an easier way to help the sick and dying.

Where does money come in? Money has been an essential part of the human experience for millennia. Aside from perhaps a few hardcore survivalists, no one can get by today without money. It's what allows us to buy food and shelter and other necessities of life. It also allows us to specialize in one area of expertise rather than spending every day just try-ing to hunt or grow food to survive. Because of money's central role in our life, many of the individual choices—in-cluding moral choices—that we make each day are related to money. Will I go to work today? Should I spend fifty dollars on a nice steak dinner tonight or only ten making bean bur-ritos so I can save the rest? Should I save some of this paycheck for my child's college fund? Should I give more to charity? How should I spend my Christmas bonus? All of these choices revolve around money.

Money isn't simply a neutral bystander with regard to morality. Often money directs us toward certain decisions, including immoral choices. If you polled people currently imprisoned, I'd bet that a desire for money figured in a major-ity of their crimes. Whether poor or rich, people tend to covet money. Even when someone has a lot of money, he desires more. We are apt to become envious when we see others with more money than we have (no matter how much we have), and we are inclined to get upset if we feel our work isn't valued (in money) as much as we think it should be.

The apostle Paul writes to his young disciple Timothy that "the love of money is the root of all evils" (1 Tim. 6:10). Paul realized that our desire for money can drive us to do many horrible things. Two of the seven deadly sins are directly connected to money: greed and envy. Money can also lead one more easily into other deadly sins, such as lust and gluttony and sloth.

Jesus understood how important money is to our lives, and he talked about the topic more than any other. Nearly fifteen percent of his teachings recorded in the Gospels address money, and eleven of his thirty-nine parables were about money or used money to teach some spiritual truth. Jesus knew how money impacts our lives, for good or for ill.

All the major religions address money's moral implications in our lives. Following the lead of Christ, the Catholic Church has through the centuries offered many teachings related to the use of money. In the past 150 years she has also given guidance on various societal economic issues, including social teachings regarding just wages, government involvement in financial systems, and market forces, to name a few. Islam condemns *riba*, or "usury": unjust monetary gains made in trade or business. Judaism encourages honesty and fairness in financial dealings. These religions recognize the reality that money is integral to our lives, for better or worse.

It isn't only money itself that influences our individual choices; the monetary *system* of which it is a part can also affect moral decision-making. We can trace through history a variety of monetary systems, and certainly some were more prone to corruption, fraud, and theft than others, whether those problems were rooted in the type of money used (stones, shells, silver, gold) or how the system was structured (banking systems, government involvement in money). Some of those systems worked more efficiently than others (there's a reason we don't use feathers as money anymore), and some made it easier to defraud and steal from others. Some systems, as we will see, were even corrupt and fraudulent in their very origins.

Most people today, however, assume the form of money we use is morally neutral, and think the problems in our economy lie elsewhere. In fact, no major religion has ever declared that any particular monetary form is either moral or immoral, or even better or worse than any other. Yet the past century has shown that certain *forms* of money—not just certain *uses* of money—can be and are immoral. Which means that some forms of money are more moral than others.

For too long people have judged monetary systems purely on utilitarian grounds: Is the money easy to transfer? Can it be divided into smaller units easily? Is it durable? These are important questions—any money that is good will also be easy to use—but usefulness should only be part of the equation when judging the morality of a monetary system. Something so integral to our lives cannot be evaluated only on the basis of efficiency; we also have to ask if the money itself fosters good behavior or bad behavior, if it unfairly favors one set of people over another, and if it defrauds certain users of the money.

It's my contention that bitcoin is the most moral money that's ever existed. It's more moral than shells or coconuts or stones or even gold or silver—and definitely far more moral than modern, government-based money such as the dollar. It also happens to be highly efficient.

These claims might sound outlandish to you right now. After all, the first practical use of bitcoin in the real world was on a website called "Silk Road" that allowed the buying and selling of illegal drugs and other black-market items. In more recent years, numerous bitcoin-related companies have been shut down and their founders even arrested for circumventing laws and regulations or for defrauding their customers. How can I say that bitcoin is the most moral money in history?

Keep reading to find out.

Chapter 1

The Eight Principles of Moral Money

*In the Old Testament a twofold attitude
towards economic goods and riches
is found. On one hand, an attitude
of appreciation sees the availability
of material goods as necessary for
life.... On the other hand, economic
goods and riches are not in themselves
condemned so much as their misuse.*

— *Compendium of the Social Doctrine
of the Church*, no. 323

SINCE THE EARLIEST times man has had a love/hate relationship with money. Money is necessary in order to obtain the material goods we need each day. Yet money — particularly the misuse of money — fosters many of the evils of this world, such as greed, envy, lust, and gluttony. All the world's major religions recognize this dualism and so offer many moral teachings related to money and the economic life of man.

Rather than detail every religion's teachings on money, I'll focus here instead on my own faith, Catholicism. Practitioners of other religions will find much overlap between the teachings of the Catholic Church on money and those of their own faith. That's because these principles are not based on any particular religion, but instead on natural law — the inherent and immutable moral principles which we can know through reason alone. Even atheists and agnostics can recognize these principles as legitimate and beneficial to humanity.

In this vein, over the centuries the Catholic Church has applied various moral teachings to new economic realities when they have arisen. Whether the topic is free-market capitalism or communism or anything in between, the Church has released teachings that evaluate these systems from a Catholic perspective. Yet, perhaps surprisingly, the Church has never explicitly declared a definitive teaching on the morality of various *forms of money*, such as gold or silver or paper or seashells. Yes, the Catholic Church, following the teachings of her Master and the Sacred Scriptures, has warned against the love of money and the dangers of excessive consumerism and consumption. But the form of money itself? On this topic Catholicism, like all major religions, has been silent.

When we examine the evolution of money and how it's used, we start to understand this apparent oversight. The vast majority of people who ever lived simply accepted the form of money they used—whether it was coconuts or feathers or silver or gold—as "the way things are." Questions of morality focused on *how* that money was used, not the form of money itself. And for thousands of years, this made sense, because the forms of money themselves were things from nature, outside the control—and moral choices—of man. The idea of an immoral money simply never registered.

Yet we'll see in this book that a new, deeply immoral form of money became prevalent in the twentieth century, but because most people accept at face value that the money they use is just part of the background of the economic landscape, the morality of that new form of money has rarely been challenged. The Catholic Church too has remained silent on this issue. If you look at the index to the *Catechism of the Catholic Church* (*CCC*), the term *money* has only a few entries, and all are related to the *use* of money, not its form, including, "idolatry and the divinizing of" and "simony." Even the *Compendium of the Social Doctrine of the Church*, a document issued by the Catholic Church in 2004 which covers economic issues extensively, has only three index entries for money itself, and they too concern only how it is used, not the form of money itself.[1]

However, Catholicism and all major religions share certain moral principles that may be applied to any situation, and so we can use these moral principles and teachings to morally assess various forms of money, including our modern monetary system—and bitcoin.

But first let us lay out those foundational principles.

RELEVANT MORAL PRINCIPLES

The principles to use when evaluating the morality of money are found in the Ten Commandments; in particular, the seventh commandment: "You shall not steal." **Theft** is the most obvious direct violation of this commandment, and any action that takes the property of another without consent is to be condemned.

Theft can take many forms: a robber can break into a house and steal a work of art, or an employee can spend his workday playing video games and thereby steal the wages his employer pays him. No matter how it's done, theft is always wrong. And when it comes specifically to the theft of money, note what it entails: it takes away the ability of a person to purchase other goods, such as food, housing, and clothing.

---

[1] The entries in the *Compendium* are titled "Public communications and the unscrupulous use of money," "The love of money," and "The debt crisis and public moneys." The *Compendium*, issued by the Pontifical Council for Justice and Peace in 2004, is available online at https://www.vatican.va/roman_curia/pontifical_councils/justpeace/documents/rc_pc_justpeace_doc_20060526_compendio-dott-soc_en.html.

Therefore, robbing someone's **purchasing power** is a violation of the seventh commandment.

Further, money is typically obtained as the **fruit of our labor**. The *Catechism of the Catholic Church* states, "Everyone has the right of economic initiative; everyone should make legitimate use of his talents to contribute to the abundance that will benefit all and to harvest the just fruits of his labor" (no. 2429).

Any action that would take away or unjustly devalue the fruit of our labor is unjust and a violation of the seventh commandment.

Another important application of the seventh commandment is the idea of a **just wage**.[2] This teaching has sparked considerable debate concerning its application in society; however, the belief that an employer should not take advantage of an employee by underpaying him is universal. But there is another aspect of a just wage that is rarely considered: What if the wage is just at the time it is received, but the value of that wage quickly shrinks in purchasing power due to the acts of some third party? After all, the underlying point of a just wage is that a person can support himself and his family on this wage; in other words, that the wage received allows him to purchase the goods needed to "provide a dignified livelihood" (*CCC*, 2434). If the value of his wages significantly decreases over time, then the worker's ability to provide a dignified livelihood decreases as well.

This brings us to the next application of the seventh commandment, the need for a **stable currency**. The *Catechism*, quoting Pope John Paul II's encyclical *Centesimus Annus*,

[2] See *CCC*, no. 2434.

states, "Economic activity ... presupposes sure guarantees of individual freedom and private property, as well as stable currency" (no. 2431).[3] A stable currency simply means that money maintains its value over time. What you can purchase for ten dollars today you can purchase for ten dollars in a year or five years. Sadly, the twentieth and twenty-first centuries have provided multiple examples of currencies devaluing rapidly in a short time, making the money almost worthless in a matter of months.

What we will see is that the instability of today's money is caused by the decisions of men. Who would choose to create monetary instability? Only those who are enriched by it. Meanwhile, the rest of the society is impoverished.

In a very real way, then, this is a form of theft. The question becomes, At what point do rising prices due to devalued money cross the threshold to theft? If ten dollars can only purchase one dollar's worth of goods in six months, that's clearly a type of theft; but what if the original value of ten dollars only decreases by 10 percent or 5 percent or 2 percent—are those levels morally acceptable? We will consider these questions going forward.

The seventh commandment also makes demands on individual choices about the use of money, and we'll see that the form of money can influence those choices. In particular, **temperance** is demanded: "In economic matters, respect for

---

[3]   Not only did Pope John Paul II (1920-2005) lead the Catholic Church for 34 years, but he was also considered a moral leader for the whole world, particularly due to his stalwart opposition to communism as well as his warnings against the excessive consumerism found in the West. He wrote extensively on moral issues, including the morality of economic systems.

human dignity requires the practice of the virtue of *temperance*, so as to moderate attachment to this world's goods" (*CCC*, no. 2407). **Excessive consumerism** is antithetical to this virtue of temperance and should be avoided.

> *The phenomenon of consumerism maintains a persistent orientation towards "having" rather than "being."* This confuses the "criteria for correctly distinguishing new and higher forms of satisfying human needs from artificial new needs which hinder the formation of a mature personality." To counteract this phenomenon it is necessary to create "lifestyles in which the quest for truth, beauty, goodness and communion with others for the sake of common growth are the factors which determine consumer choices, savings and investments."[4]

If a form of money by its very nature encourages consumerism, then that form of money can be considered morally deficient. Likewise, if a form of money encourages temperance and discourages consumption, then it can be seen as more moral in nature.

Money impacts all aspects of human life, including the family. Parents have a duty to provide for their children: "Parents' respect and affection are expressed by the care and attention they devote to bringing up their young children and *providing for their physical and spiritual needs* (*CCC*, no. 2228, emphasis in original).

---

[4] *Compendium of the Social Doctrine of the Church*, no. 360, quoting *Centesimus Annus*; emphasis in original.

We can see here that the parents' duty extends beyond just providing for the family's spiritual needs; they must also provide for their *physical* needs, which means any form of money that makes it more difficult to provide for one's family, either by becoming devalued over time or by fostering a spirit of excessive and irresponsible spending, would be morally inferior to one that does not.

Finally, another important aspect of morality when it comes to economic matters is a **care for the poor**.

> God blesses those who come to the aid of the poor and rebukes those who turn away from them: "Give to him who begs from you, do not refuse him who would borrow from you"; "you received without pay, give without pay." It is by what they have done for the poor that Jesus Christ will recognize his chosen ones. (*CCC*, no. 2443)

Any form of money that prefers the rich over the poor or punishes the poor to further enrich the well-connected should be considered immoral.

As we explore the various historical forms of money and our modern form of money, as well as this new form of money called bitcoin, we need to keep the above moral principles in mind:

- ✢ Theft of someone's purchasing power is always condemned.
- ✢ We have a right to the fruit of our labor.
- ✢ Workers should receive a just wage.

✠ Economies should have a stable currency.

✠ Temperance should be encouraged.

✠ Excessive consumption should be discouraged.

✠ Parents must be able to provide for their families.

✠ Societies should care for the poor.

If a form of money fails to support these things, it can be considered immoral, and if it encourages them, then it can be considered moral from a natural law perspective.

Admittedly, the idea of "immoral" or "moral" money might still sound very strange; does this mean I have committed a sin if I simply use an immoral form of money? No; what we're talking about are *systemic* moral issues in which the structures of an economic system, based in the form of money being used, foster either morality or immorality. When we apply the principles we've laid out in this chapter, we'll see that various forms of money can be graded on particular criteria such that we can consider some far more moral than others.

Chapter 2

The Seven Properties of Moral Money

Bread is made for laughter,
and wine gladdens life, and
money answers everything.

—Ecclesiastes 10:19

MOST BELIEVERS WON'T generally list "money" as a favorite conversation topic. With every religion warning of the dangers of money and Christ's teaching that it's harder for a rich man to enter Heaven than a camel to go through the eye of a needle, money seems at best a necessary evil, and at worst the root of all evil (a misinterpretation of 1 Timothy 6:10, which says "the *love* of money is the root of all evils").

While it's true that money can be morally dangerous, the existence of money makes our world a better place to live. Without money, we would have very few artists or musicians or philosophers—imagine a world without Beethoven or Van Gogh or Aristotle. That would be our world without money. To understand why this is the case, we need to understand the purpose of money and how it came to be. Doing so will also let us judge the usefulness and morality of different forms of money, including bitcoin.

The key characteristic of our fallen world is **scarcity**. We do not have everything we want, and sometimes not even everything we need. If I desire ten thousand apples, they won't just appear out of nowhere; they will cost something in time and resources. In other words, I need to trade something I have—whether it's my energy or my current resources—in order to receive the ten thousand apples. And my energy and resources are limited—if I give them up for apples, I can't then give them up for oranges or Teslas. Even the super-rich, such as Elon Musk, can't have everything they want. Scarcity and the trade-offs that result from scarcity rule this world.

How do I obtain the things I need and the things I want? If I live on a deserted island, I have to work for each one. My energy and time are traded for goods, such as coconuts and shelter. There's no need for money in this "Robinson Crusoe economy."

If I live in a very small and primitive village, I also likely won't need money. In our village we subsist by farming or hunting and we can share our resources with each other (while perhaps removing any member of the village who refuses to work alongside us).

In both of these cases, however, life is very hard. Almost all time is spent just trying to survive. No one will have much time—or much use—for painting beautiful works of art or composing symphonies or contemplating the mysteries of the human condition. Each day is filled with one question: How do I make it through the day?

DIRECT EXCHANGE: BARTER

Now imagine a larger group of people, perhaps three or four villages consisting of ten thousand people. Due to the size of the society, the people can begin to engage in specialization. A few families can be farmers while others are hunters and others are responsible for building shelters. This allows each family to become more efficient in their respective tasks, thus freeing up time for leisure and other nonessential activities.

But we have a problem: How do we fairly distribute the goods between the various families? How do we make sure the farmer has a shelter and the hunter has corn and the house-maker has both meat and corn? The first solution to this issue in history was barter, the **direct exchange** of goods between people.

Farmer Alan trades a hundred ears of corn for fifteen pounds of deer meat. Hunter Bob trades 150 pounds of deer meat for a house. And homebuilder Charlie trades a house for a thousand ears of corn. Everybody can be fed and sheltered without each person having to do all the work for himself.

Direct Exchange (Barter)

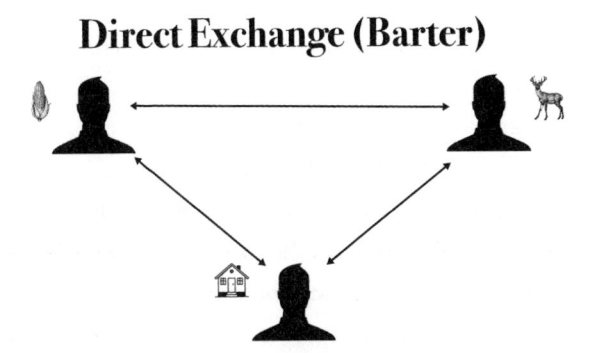

Of course, it's pretty clear how inefficient this system is. What if Charlie doesn't need a thousand ears of corn but only wants a hundred? Does he trade one-tenth of a house to Alan? And after Alan and Bob barter for their houses, they won't need another one for years, but Charlie will continue to need both meat and corn.

INDIRECT EXCHANGE: MONEY

This is where money comes in. Recognizing the inefficiency of exchanging any and all goods and services directly, people naturally began to see that one or two goods were valued by a wide segment of people. For example, perhaps everyone values topaz stones; maybe they have a superstitious value or perhaps everyone in the community believes them to be particularly beautiful. Plus, the supply of topaz stones is relatively small and the stones are particularly convenient to store and keep in one's possession. The topaz stones become a **store of value**.

Note that "value" is a subjective, intangible idea. One culture may value topaz stones, another might value rubies, while a third might value a certain bird's feathers. It's not as if there's physical value packed into those items; instead, people decide on their own and also collectively that they consider them worth owning. Nor is it just because they are rare: plenty of goods in nature are rare, such as ice in a desert area or sand in a jungle. Why a culture determines what exactly is the best store of value is determined by many factors, although we will see that a set of specific properties led to certain goods being accepted as stores of value around the world.

Because the topaz stones are considered valuable by a large segment of the population, everyone is willing to trade their goods for them. The topaz stones now become the means of **indirect exchange**: I trade my corn for your topaz stones, and you can later trade those topaz stones (plus more you have received elsewhere) for a house. So a topaz stone has become a **medium of exchange** that is not consumed itself but is used primarily in exchange for other goods. It's used in indirect, rather than direct, exchanges. Over time a topaz stone may no longer be valued for the original reasons (superstition, beauty, etc.) but only as the means by which other goods can be obtained.

Once a good is established as a store of value and used more and more for indirect exchanges, it may eventually become the *primary* medium of exchange. At this point, the good also becomes a **unit of account**; in our example, all goods and services will be priced as a certain number of topaz stones.

Perhaps in these villages a hundred ears of corn is worth one topaz stone; ten pounds of venison is worth two topaz stones; and a house is worth ten topaz stones. Now, when Alan and Bob and Charlie (and everyone else in the villages) want to exchange goods, they just buy and sell them for topaz stones. Alan and Bob can save their topaz stones to eventually buy a house, while Charlie will have topaz stones from his house sales that can be used for a long time.

The arrangement assumes, of course, that a topaz stone is not only valued by everyone in the community but also that it retains its value over time. If the value of a topaz stone were to rapidly decrease for some reason, then Charlie's savings of topaz stones won't be worth as much as when he obtained them. Being a good store of value means not only that people value it today, but that over time it retains that value.

Indirect Exchange (Money)

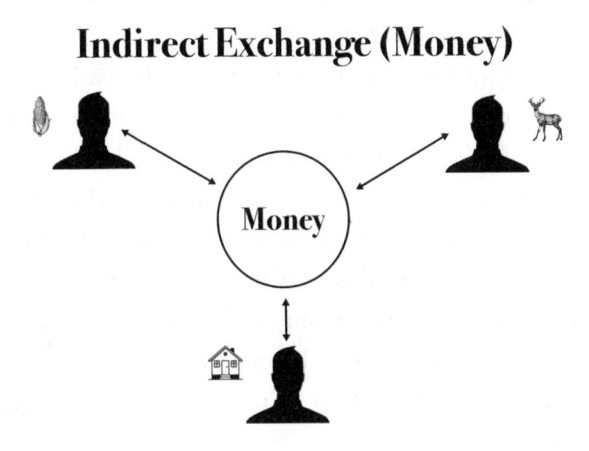

Historically, goods became money not through some top-down decision by a leader or a government but through a "spontaneous order" that developed naturally among a group of people. No tribal leader said, "You must accept topaz stones as money"; instead an organic development resulted from many exchanges made over a long period of time.

This example of the topaz stones represents how various forms of money evolved in various places and at various times throughout history. It reveals that inherent to money are three purposes:

✣ Store of Value: a good that is considered valuable and holds that value over time.

✣ Medium of Exchange: a good that is obtained not to be consumed or in the production of another good but primarily in exchange for other goods.

✣ Unit of Account: the ability to have goods and services priced as units of the money in question.

Throughout history many different goods have been used as money, and some were better than others. Sometimes a good like a seashell or sugar was used as money but subsequently got replaced because it became less valuable or lost its value altogether. Let's say someone from a village a hundred miles away comes to this group of villages and sees that they are using topaz stones. The visitor knows that back where he lives there are an abundance of them. So he goes back and grabs hundreds of these stones and returns, flooding the market with topaz stones by buying everything he can. The result of this event is that the value of topaz stones is drastically reduced.

The visitor's actions could lead to other problems, too. With the lower value of each topaz stone, more are required for each purchase. If Charlie now needs to sell his homes for a hundred stones instead of ten (due to each stone being worth less), he also needs to store and transport a lot more stones than before. Due to the flooding of the market with a large quantity of topaz stones, topaz is no longer a good store of value in this community. This can have dire consequences for the entire economy, particularly for those people who saved many topaz stones, assuming they would keep their value over the long term.

Or, instead of a market-flooding visitor, let's say raiders come to the village and steal half of all the topaz stones. Now each individual topaz stone is more valuable than before. This makes it a better store of value, but now it's not as good of a unit of account. Why is that? Before, it took one topaz stone to buy a hundred ears of corn, and now it only costs half a topaz stone. How do I buy a hundred ears if I have no way to cut a topaz stone in half? (Topaz is a very hard stone.)

THE PROPERTIES OF MONEY

Over time, people began to recognize that certain goods were better forms of money than others. These goods' value could not easily be changed by outside forces, and it could be maintained over a long period of time. Some items, such as shells, stones, feathers, and teeth, were used for a while but eventually failed as money. Other items, such as gold and silver, stuck around and continued to be used as money over the long term. Economists have studied why some items succeeded as money and why others failed. They found that the items that "stuck" as money had seven properties in particular.[5] The better a form of money ranked in these seven properties, the more likely it was to be used and to persist. And just as there was no top-down implementation of the conversion of a good to money, these properties were not something decided by an authority such as a government or a monarch. They were part of a "spontaneous order" that developed organically over time. The more useful a good was as money, the more it was used as money.

The seven properties of money can be further broken down into two categories: the first four properties make a money *useful and efficient,* and the other three properties make it *moral,* meaning it minimizes widespread and systemic theft, fraud, and corruption. The most lasting forms of money typically rank high in all seven properties.

What are the first four properties of money, the properties that make a form of money useful and efficient?

1. Money must be **divisible**. This means it can be subdivided into various amounts that are suitable for different sizes of purchase. For example, gold can be molded into various sizes and shapes, from a one-tenth-ounce coin to a kilogram bar or even larger. The Maasai people of East Africa used live cattle as money. Perhaps this didn't catch on in the rest of the word because it cannot be divided into smaller units.

2. Money should be **portable**. It should be easy to move across distances, which means it must hold a

---

[5] Historically, only the first six properties of money were proposed, but modern forms of money (which we'll look at in the next chapter) showed that the seventh property was also vital.

lot of value in a small package. At one time large Rai stones, weighing as much as eight thousand pounds, were used as money in primitive cultures on Pacific islands. Again, it's easy to see why, on a large geographic scale, that wouldn't stick. Money that can be carried in your pocket is more acceptable to people than money you cannot.

3. Money should be **durable**. It does not rot or rust or break easily, so that it can be saved over time without concern for its fragility. Seashells break easily, which is one thing that makes them not so great as money. A stone or a precious metal that does not decay makes better money in terms of durability.

4. Money should also be **fungible**. This means that individual units of money don't differ significantly from each other; one is as good as any other. For example, one ounce of gold is worth the same as any other ounce of gold. (An ounce of gold can be enhanced in some way to make it worth more, as when a government creates a special coin out of an ounce of gold. Gold is still fungible, though, because the added value comes from the added services applied to the ounce, not the ounce itself.) Some historical forms of money rated poorly on the fungibility scale. When the Maasai used livestock as money, for example, it was not fungible, since one cow might be very different from another cow.

Any form of money that ranks high in these first four properties will be efficient to use. But efficiency isn't the only requirement for good money. Certain forms of money by their very nature make systemic theft, fraud, and corruption more likely. The better a money is, the more it reduces the likelihood of these immoral practices. So, not only must money be efficient, it must be *moral*. Properties five through seven describe the criteria for a money's morality.

5. Money should be **verifiable**. A seller of goods or services must be able to check that the money really is what it appears to be. Counterfeiting should be difficult to accomplish and/or easy to spot. If creating fake money is a breeze, then immoral practices more freely abound. Ideally, a merchant would be able to verify that money is legitimate at the point of sale.

6. Money should also be **scarce**. This means it should be difficult to increase the total money supply. Many primitive forms of money became devalued because they were too easily debased when outsiders injected new money into the local economy. Consider again the stranger who brings hundreds of new topaz stones to the village; he can flood the market and decrease the value of the stones. Scarcity makes a form of money less likely to fall prey to people trying to corrupt the money supply for their own benefit.

7. Finally, money should be **independent**. It should not be controlled by any one person or entity (government, corporation). A money supply that is controlled by a small group of people invites corruption. Imagine a village in which topaz stones were the form of money, but a single council of three men controlled the entire

supply of stones. Their power over the community would be virtually unlimited.

We divided these criteria into two categories, and the best forms of money excel in both: they are useful (efficient) and moral. They rank high on all seven properties.

Now, when I call a money "moral," I am not suggesting that it thereby can't be used for immoral activities. Because we live in a fallen world, it's impossible to prevent all forms of theft and fraud and corruption, no matter the form of money used. However, moral money can make it more difficult to institute *systemic* theft, fraud, and corruption. Moral money is less prone to manipulation and control by small groups of people. It reduces and may even eliminate systemic immoral issues with the money itself.

Now that we've seen what makes a money both useful and moral, the reason gold has been used as money in most societies throughout history should be clear. It ranks high in all seven categories (although it does have some weaknesses).

Look at the advantages gold's natural properties give it:

- ✠ easily shaped into divisible parts
- ✠ relatively easy to transport (at least smaller units)
- ✠ durable
- ✠ one ounce of gold is worth the same as any other ounce
- ✠ easy to verify as real
- ✠ relatively scarce
- ✠ not controlled by any one entity.

Some people mistakenly believe that the use of gold as money happened by chance. They think that some other good, say copper, could just as easily have been widely used as money. Or that gold was probably only used because people liked it as jewelry. But the reality is that gold has naturally been the most popular form of money not by chance or whim but because it ranks high in the seven properties of money.

Why isn't gold used anymore? One reason is that the weakest monetary property of gold is portability, and a global economy demands portable money. But more importantly, modern governments took advantage of that weakness to sideline gold as the dominant form of money, because they wanted total control of the money supply and couldn't get it with gold. It's too hard to corrupt. So they replaced it with something else.

Before we dive into bitcoin and why it is superior to gold in both usefulness and morality, we need to examine how governments replaced gold, and why the new form of money they created was far more immoral than any form of money ever used. After that we'll see why bitcoin, not gold, is the path forward.

Chapter 3

The Devolution of Money

*The root and source of all monetary evil
is the government's monopoly on money.*

— Nobel Prize–winning economist
Friedrich Hayek[6]

[6] Friedrich A. Hayek, *Denationalisation of Money — The Argument Refined: An Analysis of the Theory and Practice of Concurrent Currencies,* 3rd ed. *(Institute of Economic Affairs,* 1990 [1976]*),* https://mises.org/library/book/denationalisation-money-argument-refined.

FOR MOST PEOPLE, the form of money they use is like the weather: it's just a fact of life, a force of nature, a part of the world we live in. Like someone from Minneapolis complaining about the cold from time to time, one might bemoan rising prices, but this reality is accepted as something that can't be changed.

We've seen that over the centuries people have used a wide array of forms of money, and, generally speaking, the best forms naturally end up being used the most. That's why gold and silver have been used as money in most societies throughout history. Yet today we don't use gold or silver; we use government-created money in paper, coin, and, now, digital forms.[7] How did this happen? Was it because these forms are naturally superior to gold and silver?

Sadly, no. We use them not because they are superior, but largely because they were imposed upon us by governments — for their own benefit.

[7] Note the difference between various digital types of money. One type of digital money is that which simply represents another form of money. This is what we are most familiar with: our digital dollars (like those in a credit card transaction) represent paper dollars. Then there is inherently digital money, such as bitcoin, that represents nothing else; digital is the form of the money. The outward type may be the same, but the underlying form is radically different, as we will see later.

THE GOLD STANDARD

Our modern system of money, which I will argue in the next chapter is deeply immoral, didn't originate with bad intentions. The strictly gold- and silver-based system that preceded it was initially altered for convenience's sake, taking advantage of the specific properties of paper (and later digital) money that are superior to precious metals. As I noted, gold and silver were the most common forms of money because they, historically, possessed most fully the seven properties of money. Yet that does not mean they were perfect. The property in which gold[8] was most lacking was **portability**.

Imagine a rich man with a hoard of gold. He may be happy to be rich, but he has a problem. Where does he store his gold? How does he secure it? He'll need to build a vault and hire security guards. If he wants to make a large purchase, how does he securely transport it to the seller of the good he wants? It wasn't easy to ship a hundred pounds of gold from France to England in medieval times, and it still isn't today.

The answer to this problem was the creation of money warehouses, also known as banks. A bank offered to store someone's gold securely for a fee, and like any warehouse, it gave back a paper note—a receipt. The receipt documented how much of the customer's gold was stored in the warehouse.

When the owner of the gold wanted to withdraw or spend his gold, he showed his paper note to the bank to prove his ownership. The paper of that note was not the money; it represented actual money. Although the monetary properties of that paper are inferior to those of gold (it is definitely not

---

[8] I'll just refer to gold alone from now on for convenience's sake, but my statements about it will generally apply to silver as well.

durable; it is not as verifiable as gold; and it is not at all scarce), using it to represent gold was convenient and could solve gold's portability issues.

As a result of the rise of banks, many members of society no longer had physical possession of their gold but rather a paper note that represented their gold. This led to the next step in the evolution of money: exchanging paper.

Let's say we have two people, Adam and Bill. Both have their gold stored at First Medieval Bank: Adam deposited a hundred ounces and Bill deposited fifty ounces. Bill is a shoemaker and Adam wants to buy a pair of shoes from Bill for one ounce of gold (they are very nice shoes!). Adam goes to First Medieval Bank and withdraws one ounce of gold to give to Bill. Later Bill goes to the same bank and deposits that ounce. Now Adam has ninety-nine ounces at First Medieval, and Bill has fifty-one. But guess what? The total balance at First Medieval didn't change.

People soon realized it would be much more convenient if Adam's and Bill's paper notes were simply modified so that when Adam bought the shoes from Bill, the amounts shown on their paper notes changed—no physical gold needed to change hands. Now Adam would have a note signifying he owns ninety-nine ounces and Bill's note would show he has fifty-one. The physical gold never leaves the bank. Even more convenient, perhaps Adam receives a hundred notes from the bank, each representing one ounce of gold, and Bill receives fifty similar notes. Now Adam just hands Bill one of his paper notes for new shoes.

Expand this to a larger economy of more people and more banks, and we can see how much more convenient paper notes representing gold could be versus using physical gold (though not in every way: a paper note can much more easily be accidentally destroyed and can also be more easily counterfeited).

Even in a relatively small economy, you might have thousands of transactions a day between hundreds of people who deposited their gold in dozens of banks. Person A using Bank One might pay ten ounces to Person B using Bank Two, and Person C using Bank Two might pay seven ounces to Person D who uses Bank One. Instead of using physical gold for each transaction, people complete their transactions using paper notes, and the two banks simply reconcile their gold stores at the end of the day (with Bank One sending Bank Two three ounces).

This, then, is a hybrid gold-paper system, which is also called a **gold standard**, since gold is the underlying standard on which the monetary system is based. Judging by the seven properties of money, is this a better system than using physical gold for every transaction? In some ways, yes (or it wouldn't have sprung up), but in other ways no.

Clearly, in terms of usefulness it's more efficient and convenient. Paper has a durability problem, but a gold-paper system is highly superior to gold alone in terms of both portability and divisibility, which offsets that weakness. Along with the ease of transporting, storing, and exchanging paper, a gold-paper system also allows people to spend in much smaller units. For example, a one-hundredth ounce of gold would be so small as to be easily misplaced, but a paper note representing the same fraction of an ounce would be no different than one representing a hundred ounces.

In terms of morality, however, a hybrid gold-paper system is clearly inferior, particularly in the properties of verifiability and independence. Prior to the modern era of advanced anti-counterfeiting technologies, paper was far easier to counterfeit than gold. How does an individual verify a paper note issued by a bank in the neighboring town, or, even worse, in another country? Physical gold from China can be easily accepted in Europe (if not so easily transported), but paper notes not so much.

And, by placing the gold in the hands of the bankers, a degree of independence is lost. If I store my own physical gold, no one can control what I do with it. But if a bank stores my physical gold, then it has power over my money. The banker could decide not to let me access the money; he could steal the gold; or he could lie about whether or not he has possession of it. By moving to a gold-paper system, efficiency was increased, but morality was decreased.

Sadly, the story of our money gets worse.

FRACTIONAL RESERVE BANKING

The next stage in the historical evolution (devolution?) of money was the invention of **fractional reserve banking**.

In time, bankers noticed something significant when it came to how the gold they held was used: most of their customers kept most of their gold in the bank most of the time.

The gold held in banks was primarily savings; the vast majority of customers rarely needed to actually withdraw their physical gold. So, if a bank held a thousand ounces of gold, only perhaps fifty to one hundred ounces of it was ever physically withdrawn on a given day, and usually the incoming deposits made up for those withdrawals. Since most transactions involved the exchanging of paper notes, not physical gold, customers had little reason to withdraw their physical gold. The vast majority of the gold just sat there, doing nothing. Why not make some money from that sitting money?

Thus was born fractional reserve banking. Instead of just warehousing money, banks offered loans and other financial services using the gold they held. If a bank held a thousand ounces, perhaps nine hundred of those ounces would be loaned out to people in need of money (even here the physical gold didn't usually leave the bank, but instead a new paper note, this time representing a loan, was created). Only a fraction of the deposits was held in reserve.

Depositors, in theory, would not be impacted, because the bank had enough gold held in reserve to safely satisfy typical requests for withdrawals. The practice even benefited the depositors, since the bank no longer needed to charge a fee for warehousing the gold; it could even pay depositors a percentage of the money it made from the loans it offered to other customers. Win-win, right?

I hope most people can see the problem.[9] What if depositors' requests for withdrawals exceeded what the bank held in reserve? After all, it's their gold, so they have a right at any time to take possession of that gold, at least in theory. This more-requests-than-deposits situation is what is known as a bank run. When bank runs happened, they usually resulted in the closure of the bank and the loss of funds by most of its depositors.

[9] There are actually many problems with fractional reserve banking, but for our purposes we'll only focus on the most obvious.

Fractional Reserve Banking
(under Gold Standard)

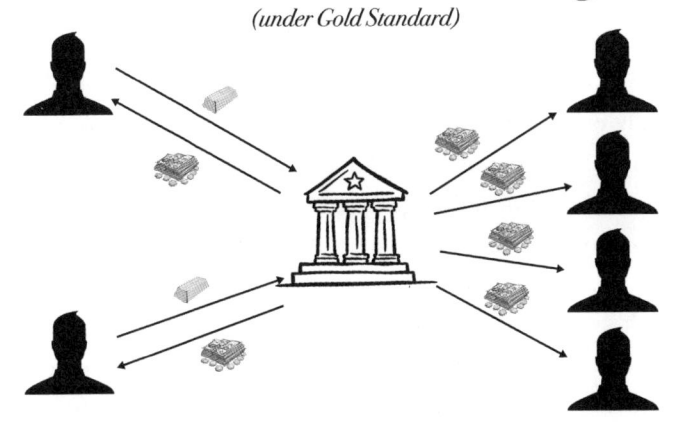

Based on the moral principles I outlined in the previous chapter, we should recognize that not only is fractional reserve banking a problem for financial reasons, but also it is deeply immoral. It is fundamentally fraudulent. Imagine you rented a storage facility today. What if the owners of that facility went into your storage area and started making extra money by loaning out the clothes and old record players and bikes you had stored there? The bank's job is to hold your money, but instead it uses it as if it were its own.

Fractional reserve banking is fraudulent in another way, too: it creates fake money.

Consider a simple economy that consists of one bank holding everyone's money. It holds a total of a thousand ounces of gold for the members of the community. In this scenario, the total money supply in that economy is one thousand ounces of gold. Now let's say that, using a fractional reserve system, the bank loans out nine hundred of those ounces to community members. What is the total money supply in this economy now—the total amount of money being used by everyone? It's 1,900 ounces of gold! That's what's available (at least in theory) for spending.

Yet we know that only 1,000 ounces of physical gold actually exist, even though there are 1,900 ounces spoken for. That extra 900 ounces is fake money—it was just created by the bank out of nothing. And not only does this mean that depositors don't actually have full access to their funds, but it also impacts the economy by raising prices: fractional reserve banking is a form of **inflation**.

Inflation, technically speaking, does not itself mean a rise in prices, as most people assume. Instead it means an increase in the money supply.[10] Whatever the origin of the increase (whether mining additional gold, loaning out fake money, or something else), the result is inflation. People assume inflation means a rise in prices, because rising prices *follow* an increased money supply as surely as daytime follows dawn, but inflation, strictly speaking, simply means more money in circulation.

Why do rising prices follow inflation? Again, let's consider a small example. A village has a total money supply of a thousand ounces of gold (there's no bank in this example; everyone holds their own gold). Ten pounds of beef costs one ounce of gold and a hundred ears of corn costs a half an ounce. But then someone discovers a large deposit of gold nearby, and soon ten thousand ounces are mined by various people in the village. Now the total money supply is eleven

---

[10] The term *inflation* has become so attached to a rise in prices in recent years that sometimes economists will distinguish between "monetary inflation" (an increase in the money supply) and "price inflation" (an increase in prices). In this book, when I refer to inflation, I am referring to the classical definition: that is, monetary inflation.

thousand ounces. With more money in the economy, people will begin to spend more; after all, what's one ounce of gold when you own one thousand? I'd like to have steak dinners every night! Soon the demand for goods increases, which leads sellers to increase their prices, since they can sell them for more than before. Inflation of the money supply—regardless of its source—leads inevitably to an increase in prices.

This chart illustrates the close connection between inflation and rising prices by plotting the increase in the money supply in the fifty years from 1960 to 2010 (dashed line) and the corresponding rise in prices during that time (solid line).[11]

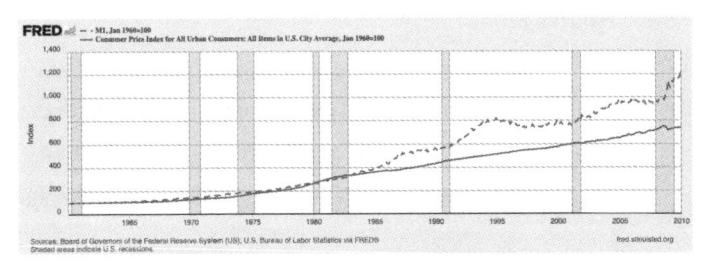

*Increases in the money supply always correlated
with a rise in prices from 1960–2010.*

The inflation plotted in the chart above is due to the creation of new money (which we will see also has dire consequences for an economy). The fractional reserve system, however, doesn't create new money. The *result* of inflation—rising prices—occurs, but not because the *actual* money supply increases. People don't have more

[11] Source: Board of Governors of the Federal Reserve System (US), M1 [M1SL], retrieved from FRED, Federal Reserve Bank of St. Louis; https://fred.stlouisfed.org/series/M1SL, March 18, 2025.

money, they are just tricked into thinking they do. Prices rise, but the people are not richer. *In terms of purchasing power, they are actually poorer.*

Today, all banks use the immoral fractional reserve system,[12] and sadly we hear very few religious leaders ever speak out against its fraudulent nature. Likely that's due to ignorance—I would guess that most people today still believe the money they deposit in the bank is actually held by that bank. But fractional reserve banking isn't even the biggest moral issue with today's money. We need to look at the next step in the evolution of our money to discover that.

FIAT MONEY

While fractional reserve banking benefited the banks, it didn't fundamentally change the gold-based monetary system. There was still scarcity of the underlying asset—it is difficult and expensive to mine new gold. So, while fractional reserve banking

[12] Today's fractional reserve banking system is actually much worse than my simple explanation above, for it contains many layers of loans, all based on fake money. First a bank loans out the initial deposits it receives, but then that new (fake) money will be deposited at another bank, which will generate more loans based on that deposit, which will generate another round of fake money, and so on. It can be confusing to understand (and hard to believe). Here's one example: assuming a 10 percent reserve rate, a $1,000 deposit would create $900 in loans. This new $900, however, is also kept in a bank—the bank of the owner of that loan. The second bank then keeps only a 10 percent reserve of that $900. It loans out the rest: $810 (90 percent of $900). The process continues: the third bank, which received that $810, creates $729 in loans (90 percent of $810), then a fourth bank creates $656.10 in loans (90 percent of $729), and so on. The initial $1,000 deposit creates close to $10,000 in additional (fake) money in the economy. It's morally and financially insane.

could inflate the money supply to some degree, there was still the restraint of the overall gold supply to keep it at least somewhat in check—a bank couldn't create unlimited fake money.

This posed a problem to a certain class of people: government officials. Governments need money to perpetuate themselves, and the primary way they raise money has always been taxation. But taxes are highly unpopular, and even powerful monarchs encountered limits to how much they could raise taxes, to say nothing of democratically elected government leaders who are beholden to the support of the people. A leader who wants to engage in an unpopular war with another country, for example, might find it difficult to raise the funds he needs solely through taxes.

One solution politicians discovered before paper dominated all transactions was physical devaluation of the currency. If a typical gold coin issued by the government with a face value of ten dollars contained a quarter ounce of gold, the government could simply start making the coin with less gold per coin without telling anyone.[13] Then more money would be available, and the difference could be kept by the government for its purposes. However, not only was this process cumbersome, it was also limited as to how much money could be generated. A better solution was needed, and the use of paper notes provided the way.

---

[13] This is actually the origin of the term "sound money." When a government snuck other metals into gold or silver coins, they would sound different when dropped on a hard surface. So citizens could determine whether or not a coin was legitimate by the sound it made. Most people would then spend the less valuable money and keep the more valuable (a principle called "Gresham's Law," which says that in any economy bad money is spent before good money).

By the early twentieth century, using paper notes to complete transactions had become the norm in the developed world. Technically those notes were all redeemable by law for gold, but people came to see the paper itself, not the underlying gold, as the money. Almost no one actually redeemed their paper for gold. Government leaders realized this and said, "Why don't we just make the paper itself our money, since people treat it like that anyway? Let's detach it from gold completely."

This paper-only money, created by government and backed only by trust in that government, is called **fiat money**. *Fiat* in Latin means "let it be done," and in this case it refers to the fact that the government is saying, "Let this money be done (created)."[14] The move to a fiat-money system occurred over decades and in America and most developed nations was essentially complete by the 1970s.[15]

---

[14] This is quite the inversion of the fiat Christians are familiar with: Mary's fiat when Gabriel told her she would be the Mother of the Savior: "Let it be done to me according to your word" (Luke 1:38). In that case, Mary was submitting to the will of God; in the case of fiat money, man acts like God, creating something (money) from nothing.

[15] Fiat money has a long and erratic history in America. Before the American Revolution, some states experimented with fiat money systems, all ending in disaster. Based on that experience, the Founding Fathers were strongly opposed to fiat money—Article I, Section 10, Clause 1 of the Constitution declared that states may not "make any Thing but gold and silver Coin a Tender in Payment of Debts." In spite of this, during the twentieth century the American government established fiat money in a staged process. Important events in this process included (1) the creation of the Federal Reserve in 1913; (2) the 1933 executive order requiring all citizens to turn in their gold; (3) the 1944 Bretton Woods Agreement, which set a fixed currency exchange rate between nations and which, in effect, made the U.S. dollar

Fiat Money Creation

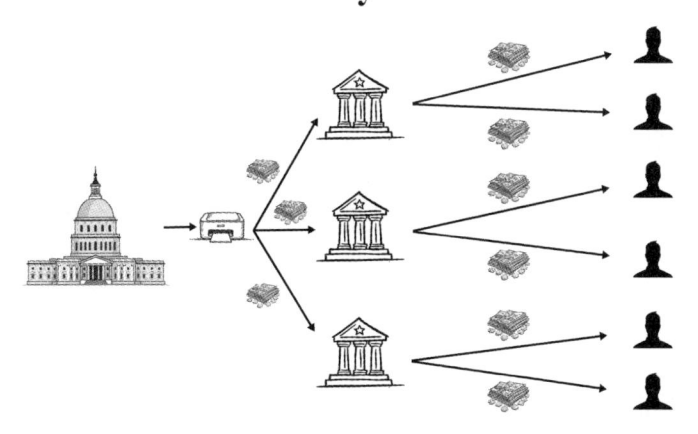

The new fiat-money system had all the same efficiency advantages as the gold-paper system: it was highly divisible, very portable, and fungible. Although paper remained poor in terms of durability, that factor diminished in importance when most fiat money went digital.

Now, however, governments could control the supply of money completely; money was no longer in any way independent. This governmental domination also meant money was not scarce, since by government decree an official could simply create new money by printing more (or adding more in a digital database). So the advent of fiat money resulted in the loss of two of the three moral properties of money.

The fiat-money system was far less moral than even the gold-paper system or the fractional reserve banking that the gold-paper system birthed. In all previous monetary systems,

the global reserve currency; and (4) the official ending of the gold standard in 1971 by President Richard Nixon.

the good used as money was something from nature — stones, coconuts, silver, gold. Money thereby had nature-imposed limits; it took time and energy to add money to the money supply. Outside of the problems of fractional reserve banking, inflation was relatively restrained and so purchasing power was maintained through time.

No one has to work in a mine to produce new fiat money. Paper is easy to create. And what's simpler than getting a government official to sign off on having more of it printed? Even the resources needed for bills and coins have been drastically reduced since the move to digital forms of money. Creating more money is as simple as adding some numbers in a database.[16]

The dramatic moral impact of this new monetary system cannot be overstated. It has influenced the moral choices of individuals and governments in far-reaching ways. In the next chapter we'll explore in depth the immorality of today's monetary system.

---

[16] It is in practice more complex than this, because governments want to give the illusion that they are not just creating money out of thin air. But the result is essentially the same.

Chapter 4

Today's Immoral Money

As a central bank, we have the ability to create money digitally. And we do that by buying Treasury Bills or bonds for other government guaranteed securities. And that actually increases the money supply. We also print actual currency and we distribute that through the Federal Reserve banks.

—Jerome Powell, chairman of the
United States Federal Reserve[17]

[17] Interview with *60 Minutes*, May 17, 2020, https://www.cbsnews.com/news/full-transcript-fed-chair-jerome-powell-60-minutes-interview-economic-recovery-from-coronavirus-pandemic/.

As should be obvious from chapter 3, the fiat monetary system is fraught with systemic moral problems. It allows a certain class of people—government leaders—to create new money whenever they need it. Want to start an unpopular war? Just print more money.[18] Need to buy votes by funding a social program? Print more money. There's no limit to the corruption possible under such a system.

Beyond this governmental abuse, the fiat-money system has other far-reaching moral consequences. Most of these consequences are hidden in plain sight today; most people are ignorant of the moral implications of fiat money.

The Decline in Purchasing Power

First, fiat money has severely reduced the average citizen's purchasing power. This is a form of theft. It's become accepted in the modern world that prices rise over time; this phenomenon is treated like a law of nature. But in reality, prices, in a free market, should generally *fall* over time. Products become easier—and therefore cheaper—to produce as people find more efficient ways to make them.

---

[18] If you look at the history of war, you see that the twentieth century witnessed the proliferation of the "total war," in which countries looked for the full and complete surrender of the opponent. Before this time wars would typically be more strategic and limited in nature. The rise of the total war occurs, not coincidently, with the rise of fiat money, in which a government could print all the money it needed to execute this type of warfare, which is far more expensive.

For example, take a loaf of bread. Due to technological advances over the years, bread is actually much easier to produce today than, say, a hundred years ago. So bread should be cheaper today than it was a century ago. Is this the case?

Actually, we find the opposite is true. Consider this chart showing how much bread a person could buy with ten dollars over the hundred-year period from 1915 to 2015.[19]

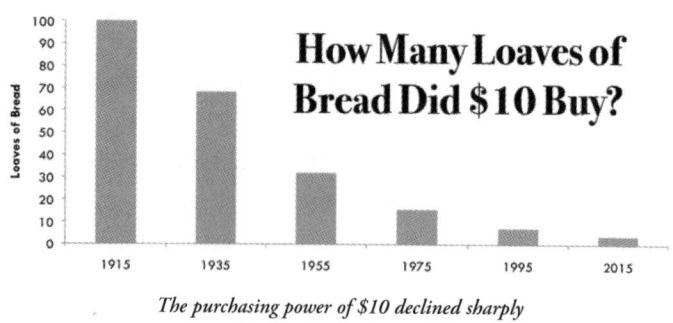

The purchasing power of $10 declined sharply in terms of loaves of bread from 1915 to 2015.

In 1915 (around when fiat money was being born in America), a person could buy a hundred loaves of bread for ten dollars. One hundred years later, in 2015, the same amount of money only got him four loaves. Is bread more expensive to produce? Have we had a century-long shortage of wheat? You might think something like that by just looking at this chart. Yet we know that producing bread hasn't become more difficult and therefore more expensive; in fact, it has become much easier. So why did the price of bread increase so much in a hundred years?

[19] Source: "Bitcoin: A Primer," ARK Invest, https://www.ark-invest. com/articles/analyst-research/bitcoin-a-primer.

Inflation of the money supply via fiat money.

Our inflation rate has been so high over the past century that falling prices that should have occurred due to technological advances have been negated by rising prices resulting from the increased money supply. Not only has inflation offset the natural price decline, it overwhelmed it so that prices for most goods rose substantially.

The technology sector makes it easy to see how lower prices over time occur naturally in a healthy economy. Because of the rapid advancement of technology over the past few decades, the cost of most technology products has gone down—the advances in technology have been so great that they have offset the inflationary rise. Most of this price decline is actually seen in improvements in the product: a PC today might cost about the same as a PC a decade ago, but it is far more powerful.

This is a normal phenomenon in all industries in a free-market economy, yet in most cases we don't see that natural price decline because it's destroyed by inflationary fiat money. Life should be getting less expensive during this age of amazing technological progress, but it's actually getting more expensive thanks to fiat money.

Consider another example: a can of Campbell's tomato soup.[20] This soup has been the same and essentially packaged in the same way for over a century. Considering the incredible

---

[20] Following an item like this tracks prices much more accurately than the conventional ways of doing so, such as the Consumer Price Index (CPI). The CPI takes a basket of goods the average American purchases and then tracks the items' prices over time. The problem is that if the price of an item in that basket rises so much that it can no longer be afforded by the average American, it is removed from the CPI basket. This of course dampens the true impact of inflation on prices. The historical price of a can

advances in technology over that time frame, it stands to reason that the price of a can of Campbell's tomato soup should have gone down dramatically. It is far easier and cheaper to manufacture it today than in the late nineteenth century. Yet, what's happened? The price has increased from around $0.10 to almost $1.30 today—a 1,100 percent increase.[21]

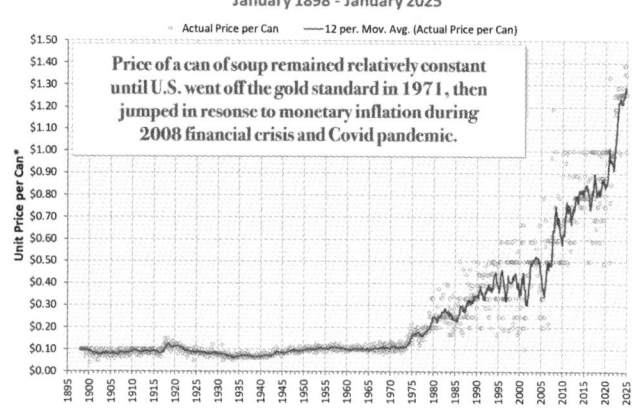

Campbell's Condensed Tomato Soup Unit Price per Can*
January 1898 - January 2025

Price of a can of soup remained relatively constant until U.S. went off the gold standard in 1971, then jumped in resonse to monetary inflation during 2008 financial crisis and Covid pandemic.

Data Sources: Selected Grocer Advertisements in U.S. Newspapers and Online, 1897-2025
* Discounted sale price of an iconic 10.75 oz. No. 1 "picnic" can of Campbell's Condensed Tomato Soup   © Political Calculations 2025

From this chart it is clear that the price of a single can of Campbell's tomato soup illustrates well the impact inflation has on prices. While the United States was still relatively tethered to the gold standard, the price of a can of soup remained constant. But when the country left the gold standard (1971),

of Campbell's tomato soup is tracked by Political Calculations: https://politicalcalculations.blogspot.com/search/label/soup.
[21] Chart source: https://politicalcalculations.blogspot.com/2025/01/the-price-history-of-campbells-tomato.html

the price of soup (along with most goods) started a steady increase as the supply of fiat money became easier to inflate. And since the only answer to financial crises in a fiat system is to print more money, we also see spikes in the price of Campbell's corresponding to the 2008 financial crisis and the 2020 COVID-19 pandemic. Once you understand the relationship between money supply inflation and rising prices in a fiat economy, this should come as no surprise.

THE DESTRUCTION OF SAVINGS

The steady and consistent price increases over time have significant consequences in the lives of most people. In a monetary system where inflation is low or nonexistent and therefore prices stay steady or even drop, saving money is very easy: simply put some of your money aside for use in the future, either at your home or in a bank if you can't secure it at your own home. If I save ten ounces of gold today, then in ten years that will still purchase around ten ounces of gold's worth of goods, or maybe more. But we know that in the fiat system this isn't true. If I put a hundred dollars under my mattress, in ten years I will only be able to purchase perhaps sixty or seventy dollars' worth of goods versus what I could buy today. The money has devalued in purchasing power over time.

This reality forces people to change their behavior in far-reaching ways. First, it encourages, even forces, people to put their savings at risk. People understand they can't just keep their money in a dresser drawer; they need to put their money to "work" just to stay even. This is not, however, how things were before the modern era, with its devaluing fiat-money system.

Let's trace the evolution of savings under fiat money. An individual's first option is a savings account at the bank, which pays a customer a rate of interest with funds derived from fractional reserve banking (but that's not a real win, since fractional reserve banking also increases inflation). At first, the rate of return keeps steady—or even outperforms—the rise in prices due to inflation. As government officials print more money, however, a savings account at the bank can't keep up. Purchasing power decreases when the rate of return is lower than the rate of inflation. In recent years savings accounts produce less than a 1 percentrate of return while the inflation rate has surpassed 5 percent—a loss of more than 4 percent of purchasing power *per year*.

When this happens, people look to other options for their savings. Perhaps a certificate of deposit (CD) or a money market account. Well, that might work for a while, but eventually these instruments can't keep up with inflation either. Bonds? Eventually bonds don't keep up.[22]

Then more people invest in stocks to stay ahead of the rising prices caused by the inflated money supply. At first most of them select boring, blue-chip stocks, but after a while even these don't offer a high enough rate of return, so the average person considers smaller, less established companies, hoping for a greater rate of return.

---

[22] From 2020 to 2022, the inflation-indexed rate of return on a 10-year treasury bond was under 0 percent—a negative rate of return. Since then (through late 2024), the return has been under 2.5 percent, but since the inflation index used is based on the CPI, which historically underestimates the true rate of inflation, it's likely that those bond returns are still under 0 percent.

What's happening here? Due to inflation, people are increasingly pushed into greater **risk**. As the potential for growth increases, so does the risk of loss. We have moved from savings to investment, and from investment to riskier and riskier investment—or, in other words, speculation.

Most people think savings and investment are the same thing, but they're not. Savings is simply putting some of your income aside for the future when you might need it in an emergency or for retirement. Investment is spending savings in order to generate future income. Perhaps you take part-ownership in a company, or buy a property in order to rent it out. Investment gives you a chance for growth, but that chance comes with inherent risk. Typically, the greater the risk attached to an investment, the greater the potential reward.

Because we live in an inflationary economy, we meld savings and investment together. But in a noninflationary environment, savings do not need to grow, they just need to be protected. They don't need to be risked in any way. After all, savings aren't intended to help someone get rich (that's what investment is for); they're simply to be there if one's income in the future goes away. Saving, then, is not supposed to be risky, or at least should hold very low risk. If you just keep your money under your mattress, there is the small risk of theft, but there's no risk of loss due to corporate mismanagement, market fluctuations, or anything of that nature. With investments, you are putting your money to "work," which means you are taking on many third-party risks beyond your control.

The average citizen, who knows little to nothing about economics or the workings of various companies, now feels compelled to risk his hard-earned money by investing—not to become wealthy, but just to do what savings would naturally do in a noninflationary economy. There's nothing innately immoral about investing, but a monetary system that *forces* a person to risk his money to provide for the future needs of his family, rather than voluntarily choosing to, is immoral. But that's what happens under inflationary fiat money.

There's a further moral issue with the forced push from saving to investments: the possibility of funding immoral practices. Today far too many corporations are involved in or support practices that are immoral. I myself at one time was unwittingly a part-owner of the company that publishes *Playboy* magazine. Here's what happened. My first job out of college offered a 401(k) plan, which, after leaving, I transferred to an IRA. I selected a mutual fund for the IRA, assuming I'd just leave it there for many years. However, about a year later I discovered that the mutual fund now included stock in Playboy Enterprises, the publishers of *Playboy* magazine. I was shocked. I wrote to the mutual fund company asking that it divest its Playboy stock. The company politely refused, so I transferred my investment away from that mutual fund. Moving forward, I realized I must remain vigilant, constantly checking to make sure none of the mutual funds or individual stocks I invested in were involved in or supported immoral activities. Needless to say, the list of such immoral companies has only grown. Doesn't it seem something has gone wrong if simply saving for one's retirement involves the possibility of accidentally funding pornography, abortion, or transgender ideology?[23]

---

[23] Because of this prevalent moral hazard, mutual funds have been created that only invest in companies that do not violate certain moral principles. For example, Ave Maria Funds "screen out

HOUSES AS INVESTMENTS INSTEAD OF HOMES

The push to chase returns and grow one's money to combat inflation reaches even into the most important purchase most people make: their homes. Historically, one's home was simply a place to provide shelter and establish a family. Today it has been financialized into an investment vehicle to "grow one's net worth."

Consider the rise of home prices over the past sixty to seventy years. In the 1950s, a family could have a single bread-winner and still afford a decent house. Today that dream is elusive for many young people. What happened?

Of course many factors contributed to this change, but one driving force was the relentless rise in home prices due to fiat money detached from any natural good such as gold. Eventually, though, people saw rising housing prices as something good, because they increased their net worth. This is an illusion. To see one's primary residence as an *investment* rather than a *home* distorts a fundamental part of establishing a family.

Rising housing prices also did the fiat powers-that-be a favor. They helped maintain the fairy tale that goes like this: "Yes, prices are rising. All my bills are going up. Heaven knows I can't buy as much bread for a couple bucks as I did a few years ago (just like that Sammons guy pointed out). But I'm ahead because my house is worth a lot more than it was a few years ago! I bought it for $200,000 ten years ago and now it's worth $250,000." Great ... except that $250,000 today is worth less in purchasing power than the $200,000 when you

---

companies that promote or support activities contrary to the core moral teachings of the Catholic Church" (avemariafunds.com/about-us/fund-family-profile.html).

originally bought the house. You might feel richer, but you're actually poorer.

By the 2000s the distorted housing market had become completely detached from reality as more and more people came to believe that real estate prices only went up. The temptation of ever-increasing home values was too good to pass up. People purchased second and third homes just for the asset appreciation. Riskier and riskier mortgages were desired, and banks, pushed by government officials, were happy to oblige. Families would buy houses far beyond their means using credit (spurred on by fractional reserve banking), and this in turn resulted in even higher prices. It was all a Ponzi scheme that originated in fiat monetary inflation.

Eventually, as we know, in 2008 the whole scheme collapsed. Millions lost their homes, which is far worse than losing on a stock or other investment, since one's home is a place to build and raise a family. It gives a sense of rootedness to children. The stresses that the loss of a home caused to countless families were immense, and underlying it all was a fiat-money system that pumped more and more money into the economy, leading to riskier and riskier investments that undermined the stability of the family.

Today, the housing market is out of reach for many young people. Whereas those in the baby-boomer generation have increased their net worth over the years due to the rising value of their homes in conjunction with inflation, those same rising prices have priced out young people, including young families looking for a place to put down roots, raise a family, and be part of a community.

CRUSHING DEBT

Our fiat monetary system is based on **debt**. We are swimming in debt—government debt, corporate debt, and personal debt (which includes mortgages, student loans, car loans, and credit cards). This is not, however, a bug in the fiat system; it is a feature. Fiat money is cheap. This might sound odd, because isn't one dollar equal to one dollar? How can it be any cheaper than that?

What I mean when I say that fiat money is cheap is that, since it can be printed or added to a digital database on a whim, it can be loaned out easily and thus cheaply. Gold has massive expenses associated with adding to the money supply, but no such costs are involved with fiat money. In fact, debt is an essential part of the process for printing new money in our economy.

How so? First, banks buy treasury bonds, which are essentially IOUs that the government issues in exchange for a loan. Then the Federal Reserve offers to buy those treasury bonds. But here's the catch: the Federal Reserve simply creates new money (usually in a digital ledger) and sends that to the banks in exchange for the treasury bonds. It costs the Fed nothing, but the banks get paid anyway—the money was cheap. New money flows into the system based on loans—money that the banks in turn will use to create commercial and personal loans.

For our system to work, we must have debt. And not a little.

As of the end of 2023, total consumer debt in America was almost $20 trillion, including $13 trillion in mortgage debt, $1.7 trillion in student loans, $1.5 trillion in car loans, and $1.3 trillion in credit card debt. Business debt totaled more than $21 trillion.[24] The average American at the end of 2023 was $104,215 in debt.[25] Inflation makes it nearly impossible to keep up with rising prices, but debt allows us to cover that problem by kicking the financial can down the road. Buy now, pay later.

Yet debt is fraught with moral problems. Proverbs 22:7 says that "the borrower is the slave of the lender." Debt is truly a form of slavery, and fiat money produces countless slaves. When a person is in debt, he is no longer free to make his own choices; he must first consider his obligations to his lender. Many young people carry the burden of significant debt and may find it a hindrance in pursuing a vocation. Most religious orders will not accept applicants who have debt. Two young adults uniting in marriage unite their debt burdens, too, and this can present real obstacles to peace and holiness in married life.

FINANCIAL NIHILISM

Inflationary fiat money also has a psychological impact on an individual's everyday spending decisions. Specifically, it encourages spending over savings. If I know my one hundred dollars today will buy only ninety-five dollars' worth of goods a year from now, I'm more likely to spend that money today.

[24] "Borrowing by Businesses and Households," *Financial Stability Report—April 2024*, Board of Governors of the Federal Reserve System, https://www.federalreserve.gov/publications/April-2024-financial-stability-report-borrowing-by-businesses-and-households.htm.

[25] "Average American Debt: Household Debt Statistics," *Business Insider*, https://www.businessinsider.com/personal-finance/credit-score/average-american-debt.

This result is actually desired by the powers-that-be, for most government and financial leaders (supported by bad economists) believe that excessive and ever-growing spending is what drives an economy. Without spending, the argument goes, our economy will not grow. Consumerism and excessive consumption, which are vices, are incentivized; government officials and economists even promote these vices as a patriotic duty.[26] Frugality and responsibility, which are virtues, are in contrast discouraged by the lords of the fiat monetary system. Yet the reality of all this spending is that people are becoming economically worse off over time, not better (not to mention the spiritual harm that consumerism and excessive consumption can cause).

This hamster wheel of excessive spending, risky investments, and debt slavery is engendering financial nihilism among the young. Decades ago, financial matters for the average family were straightforward: work hard, spend less than you make, save the rest at the bank, and you'll be able to support your family and be prepared for retirement. Now, however, young people face the daunting task of trying to keep their heads above water as prices rise exponentially (especially home prices) while what they've saved actually decreases in purchasing power.

No astute young person even considers a bank's "savings" account a vehicle for savings anymore. Instead, they must be well-versed in 401(k)s, IRAs, brokerage accounts, P/E ratios,

---

[26] After the 9/11 attacks, President Bush didn't call for sacrifice; he called for shopping. "George W. Bush 9/11 Address to the Nation," American Rhetoric, https://www.americanrhetoric.com/speeches/gwbush911addresstothenation.htm.

corporate earnings calls, and stock technical analysis. All to simply chase a rate of return that beats inflation. No wonder many of the young are tempted to despair of ever being able to have a family, not to say a large family.

This inability to keep up with fiat-money inflation has even influenced our societal demographics. Decades ago, it was commonplace for families to have only one breadwinner (typically the husband); one income was sufficient to live a comfortable life, with a decent house and a car, and with a larger average family size as well. This is far more difficult today. Most young families feel it is necessary to have two incomes to support themselves; the average family size is almost 20 percent smaller than in 1940; and many young people today rent because they simply cannot afford to buy a house at today's prices. While renting can be a viable option for many, renting makes it more difficult for a family to set down roots as a stable part of a parish and community. There are many economic and social reasons for this shift, of course, but there's no question that a major factor is the rapidly increasing cost of living brought about by fiat-money inflation.

Anyone who cares about the future of the human race should be concerned about the moral implications of this trend. In the first pages of the Sacred Scriptures God tells Adam and Eve to "be fruitful and multiply" (Gen. 1:28); a primary purpose of marriage is to bring children into the world and raise and educate them. Yet the strain caused by the decreasing value of fiat money leads many families to postpone having children, to have fewer children, or to have no children at all.

In 1971 the United States went completely off the gold standard. That year the average age of mothers having their first child was about 21.5 years old. In 2022, it was 27.5—six years older.[27] Obviously, the temptation to delay or avoid pregnancy makes the use of immoral methods of birth control more likely. Again we see how a monetary system can have far-reaching moral implications for the individuals who live under it.

The Well-Connected Get Richer

If the terrible effects of inflation caused by immoral money printing are not bad enough, there's yet another problem: the Cantillon effect. This is the reality, first recognized by eighteenth-century French economist Richard Cantillon, that new money distributed into an economy is not distributed equally. Those who are closest to the money benefit the most.

Earlier I noted that an increase in the money supply—inflation by the strictest definition—results in an increase in prices. But this doesn't happen immediately; it takes time. Consider again our previous example. A large amount of gold is found near a village. When the miners of this new gold make their first purchases, it has little impact on prices—it's not as if all the other merchants in the village immediately recognize what's going to happen. But as the miners continue to purchase items, it creates a ripple effect. That new money they inject into the village's economy works its way through,

---

[27] Paxtyn Merten, "Here's How the Average Childbirth Age Has Changed over Time," Northwell Health, July 30, 2024, https://www.northwell.edu/news/the-latest/geriatric-pregnancy-increases-complication-rate.

until prices begin to steadily rise throughout the village. The miners in this scenario are the ones closest to the new money, so they are the ones who can take advantage of the delay in the rise of prices.

And who is closest to the new money today? Typically banks, large corporations, and those connected to the government.

When the American government injects money into the economy, the first people to benefit are those who first receive the money, which is typically banks and corporations with government contracts.[28] They have new money at the old prices. But once that new money works its way into the economy, the average American has received very little of it but must still deal with new, higher prices for most items.

Wages in particular lag the inflationary impact on prices, for a variety of reasons. One of the main ones is that an increase in wages is typically permanent, but the typical company cannot be sure whether the latest rise in prices is temporary or permanent, so it delays increasing wages for its workers. Further, most companies are not Amazon, Lockheed Martin, or Microsoft. They are downstream from the new money and so don't themselves benefit from the Cantillon effect, making it difficult for them to pass those benefits on to their employees.

When new money is injected into a fiat-money economy, then, the rich typically get richer and the poor (and middle-class) get poorer. Income disparity skyrockets. There's a reason most people associated with the government and the banking

---

[28] Note that, according to the 2020 U.S. Census, five of the seven richest counties in America surround Washington, D.C.

system don't oppose a fiat monetary system: whether they consciously recognize it or not, it benefits them at the expense of everyone else—another reason for rising financial nihilism among the young.

CULTURAL IMPACTS

I've focused mostly on the economic inflationary effects of a fiat monetary system, but money directly controlled by governments also has other negative consequences. For starters, let's look at how this control has a chilling effect on free speech and free association, especially in the digital age.

If government controls the money, then government controls the banks. And banks control the money of the masses. By the transitive property it is clear that government's power over the individual citizen in a fiat monetary system far outweighs what they've enjoyed at any other time in history.

Proponents of fiat argue this control is necessary today to stamp out nefarious activities such as terrorism and drug dealing. Yet those things continue; meanwhile, in order to silence dissent, the government forces the "debanking" of innocent people. For example, during the 2022 Canadian trucker protest—a protest that was peaceful and legal—government officials froze the funds donated to the movement and shut down the bank accounts of its prominent members. Since our money mostly consists of entries in a computerized database controlled by banks (a highly efficient system, it must be admitted), accomplishing this injustice was child's play.

This power jeopardizes all types of debate or dissent. Modern culture is determined to control speech, and its go-to move is "canceling" people. Is there any more efficient way to frighten people into submission than threatening their bank accounts? People of faith in particular should be sensitive to this threat, as we often hold beliefs and values contrary to the dominant culture and its powerful elites.

Government control of money can also result in the theft of funds due to government and/or banking mismanagement and corruption. In 2013, the nation of Cyprus faced a severe financial and banking crisis due to decades of economic mismanagement. In response, the Bank of Cyprus announced a 47.5 percent "haircut" on deposits over €100,000 as part of an international financial bailout for the country.[29] This meant that 47.5 percent of those deposits were converted into equity to save the bank. In other words, the bank stole 47.5 percent of all funds in accounts over €100,000. If you held your life savings in the bank, it was now cut almost in half, and there was nothing you could do about it.

THE IMPACT OF WAGE SLAVERY

Rising prices caused by our inflationary fiat monetary system also deeply impact career choices, especially those of young people. Many people today must work a job — or multiple jobs — they don't like simply to keep up with rising prices. Before America went off the gold standard, a man could work a modest blue-collar job, be the primary breadwinner for his family, purchase a house without going into incredible debt,

---

[29] "Cyprus Central Bank Announces 47.5 Percent Haircut on Large Bank of Cyprus Deposits," Reuters, July 30, 2013, https://www.reuters.com/article/markets/cyprus-central-bank-announces-475-percent-haircut-on-large-bank-of-cyprus-depos-idUSL6N0G0331/.

and still put some money aside for the future. There wasn't pressure to chase after the highest-paying jobs.

Not so today. Salary has always been a factor in a decision to take a job, but now it's the primary driver. "How much will I make?" becomes the chief concern. While in some cases this might be a result of greed, I'd wager that in most situations it's simply a matter of trying to stay ahead of the ever-increasing cost of living. Most families today feel they must have two wage-earners. And individuals will work two jobs, not to make a fortune, but to continue to put food on the table, a roof over their heads, and clothes on their kids. Imagine, however, a world where prices were not constantly rising and putting aside a little each month was enough to be financially secure. In that world (which very few people living today have ever experienced), people can choose careers less for the salary level and more for fulfillment.

This particularly has an impact in the nonprofit sector; For example, a young person who wants to help others is instead working all day in a cubicle for a faceless company to pay the rent rather than working for a nonprofit assisting those less fortunate. Or someone with musical talent never gets to reach his full potential because he is a slave to his constantly devalued money. Fiat money doesn't just impact money; it impacts the world.

A Problem Hidden in Plain Sight

Given all the assaults on morality of our current monetary system, why don't we ever hear condemnations of it from our religious leaders? We rightly hear condemnations of other systemic injustices such as racism and abortion; why not address the injustices of fiat money and inflation? And since it disproportionately harms the poor, shouldn't the care for the poor that many religions proclaim lead more people of faith to speak out against it?

Sadly, I think we hear nothing because most people don't realize that there are other monetary system options. And they don't see that the fiat system's worst flaw—inflation—is a silent form of theft. If a government official were to break into your house and steal some of your money, it would be clear that his act was immoral. Inflation, however, steals our money behind our backs. The fact that people simply accept rising prices as normal makes it easy. It's commonplace for older people to talk about the price of a gallon of milk when they were young. "Remember when a gallon of milk was only two bucks? Remember when gas was under a dollar a gallon? Those were the days." But no one thinks to ask, Why did the prices of milk and gas go up so much? Can we do anything to prevent these constantly rising prices, or are we just fated for one-hundred-dollar gallons of milk some day?

In a way, this makes our current fiat monetary system even more immoral. The undisguised thief who walks up to you in broad daylight and takes your money is bad, but at least you know you've been robbed and who did it. The government official who siphons purchasing power out of your bank account—without you even noticing it and under the cover of the law—is far worse.

We should all oppose this injustice. Yet it is so pervasive and so accepted that even those who recognize its immorality often feel helpless to prevent it. After all, what can be done?

A few people advocate returning to a gold-paper system or even a fully gold system. The problem is that gold-paper systems inevitably lead to fiat money, and a fully gold system just can't work due to its poor portability—it inevitably leads to a gold-paper-digital system (a gold standard). And a gold standard just as inevitably leads to a fiat system, because once officials are empowered to create a form of currency, such as paper/digital, that they can control even in part, eventually they create a form they can completely control (thank you, fallen human nature). This pattern has been repeated throughout the world for the past 150 years. If we want moral money, we need a whole new monetary system.

Happily, a solution was proposed in October 2008. The world was in the throes of a financial implosion, caused mostly by the immoral fiat monetary system. The powers-that-be had the same solution to the crisis as always: print more money and bail out the members of the Cantillon class. This would cover up the problems at least until the next election, but it would also make the immoral systemic issues even more entrenched in the long term.

But someone else—someone outside the corridors of power and with no institutions to support him—conceived of another solution: What if we combine the moral properties of gold (and maybe even improve upon them) with the advanced usefulness and efficiency of the modern digital fiat monetary system (without its flaws) and create an entirely new form of money? The idea was grandiose in scope, and perhaps even a bit insane. Yet propose it he did, and the idea eventually caught fire.

That person was Satoshi Nakamoto, and his solution is called bitcoin. Let's turn to that ingenious and moral monetary system now.

Chapter 5

How Bitcoin Works

I've been working on a new electronic cash system that's fully peer-to-peer, with no trusted third party.

—Satoshi Nakamoto[30]

[30] "Bitcoin P2P e-cash paper," email posted to the Cryptography Mailing List, October 31, 2008, as archived at the Satoshi Nakamoto Institute, https://satoshi.nakamotoinstitute.org/emails/cryptography/1/.

On October 31, 2008, a person or persons going by the name "Satoshi Nakamoto" posted a white paper to an online cryptography mailing list describing "a new electronic cash system that's fully peer-to-peer, with no trusted third party." He called this new system "bitcoin."[31]

Satoshi was not the first to attempt to create an electronic cash system—fully digital money. A movement of activists called "cypherpunks" had been advocating for electronic cash systems dating back to the 1980s. Such systems would use strong cryptography to allow for secure, private transactions on the internet, outside the control of governments or banks. Some of these cypherpunks attempted to create such a system, but they all failed for one reason or another.

First, it was technically challenging to pull off. It's easy to say, "Let's build digital money," but a lot harder to actually create it. Since digital files are easy to create and to copy, a fully digital monetary system would need to overcome this

[31] "Satoshi Nakamoto" is assumed to be a pseudonym, and to this day the identity of this person (or group of persons) is unknown. It's an extraordinary mystery, considering how widespread bitcoin has become and the purported worth of Nakamoto, who is believed to own one million bitcoin, although no coins associated with him have ever been spent. For the purpose of convenience, I will refer to Satoshi as an individual man.

Read the full white paper, "Bitcoin: A Peer-to-Peer Electronic Cash System," at https://bitcoin.org/bitcoin.pdf. It's only nine pages and relatively easy to understand.

property so that money could not be created by just anyone and copied between users.

The second difficulty was the issue of control. We've seen that fiat money is controlled by governments and the banks, which means it fails when it comes to the vital monetary property of *independence*. The government decides when money is created and how much money is created, and banks approve transactions between participants in the system, which leads to all sorts of moral problems.

Most of the early attempted electronic cash systems ended up being managed in a centralized fashion—a private company verified all transactions and determined the money supply. However, creating a digital money system in which a corporation or a person controls both the creation of money and its flow does not solve the problem of the independence of the money; it just transfers control to another entity. Further, any entity that creates a centralized system will quickly enter the sights of the government, which does not appreciate competition when it comes to creating money. The few electronic cash systems that did include centralized control by a private entity were soon shut down (and in some cases their developers arrested).

In light of these failures, Satoshi realized that what was needed was a secure and truly independent digital money; that is, one that did not require its users to have trust in any centralized authority. Trust is essential to a fiat system, but sadly that trust is often broken. Satoshi wanted to remove the need to trust any third-party entity, and his white paper described a way to design this kind of secure, independent digital money.

But not only did Satoshi propose an electronic cash system, he built it. Only two months after releasing the bitcoin white paper, on January 3, 2009, he released the first version of the software to the internet.[32] And so was born the greatest and most moral monetary system in history.

BITCOIN BASICS

But what exactly is bitcoin? How does it work?

For most people, it doesn't really matter how it works. Most people don't understand how email works, but they send emails to their friends, family, and coworkers every day. Most of us don't understand how many of the things we use in modern life—from cell phones to microwaves to artificial intelligence (AI)— actually work. We just know that they do, and we know how to operate them.

But when it comes to a revolutionary new monetary system that claims to be as well-designed as Satoshi and other bitcoin proponents claim it to be, it's understandable that people want at least a basic understanding of how it works. Some of the details of how bitcoin works are vital to understanding why it is a more moral system than fiat. If, for example, bitcoin claims to be independent but underneath the hood is actually quietly controlled by some entity, its claim of independence is invalidated. If it claims to be scarce, but there's a secret way to pump up the money supply, then it's not a scarce form of money. So

---

[32] It is believed that he began work on bitcoin in 2007 and didn't publish the white paper until it was almost complete. We know bitcoin wasn't in production before January 3, 2009, since Satoshi encoded a message in the first block, containing the words, "The Times 03/Jan/2009 Chancellor on brink of second bailout for banks," which was a front-page headline that day in the *London Times*.

we need to know the basics of how bitcoin works in order to evaluate its morality. In this chapter I'll start with a basic overview and then move to a more detailed technical outline. If you get a little lost in some of the technical details, don't worry. Just aim to understand the big picture.

In a nutshell, bitcoin is a way to transfer value over the internet in a trustless manner. It can be compared to email; email, like bitcoin, transfers information over the internet, and in the case of email, it typically transfers text, graphics, and videos. When you send an email to a friend, your email software takes the content of the email, wraps it in a digital packet, and then sends it off into the internet. The internet consists of thousands upon thousands of computers (called servers) connected to each other, and your email jumps along those servers until it finds its home on the server that hosts your friend's email account. From there, your friend can download his mail to his email program on his computer or other device. The routing of that email — and the billions of other emails being sent each day — is controlled by software running "protocols," or rules for how to direct email over the internet.

Hopefully I haven't lost anyone yet. Bitcoin works in much the same way as email. When someone sends bitcoin from his wallet to another person's wallet, the bitcoin software broadcasts that transaction out to the internet, to be relayed along computers running the bitcoin software until it reaches its destination.[33]

---

[33] This isn't a precisely accurate description of how bitcoin works, and I'll explain it more fully later in this chapter, but this description allows us to continue the analogy with email for now.

Sounds simple, right? But perhaps you've already realized the difference between digitally sending an email consisting of text, graphics, and video and digitally sending *money*. If I receive an email, I can forward that email to another person, or I can copy and paste the text into another program and manipulate it however I please. All the while the email also remains on my device. If someone sends me an image, that image now resides on both his computer and mine—and I can send it to countless other people. But we don't want people to be able to do that with money! If I send someone one BTC (the abbreviation for the unit of money in bitcoin), it would be a disaster if he could just copy that one BTC over and over and spend it however he wants. That would be a fiat inflationary system, where everyone is his own government, printing money to his heart's desire!

So the first genius aspect of bitcoin is Satoshi's solution to this "double-spend" problem. Satoshi designed the system so that there is no way to copy bitcoin and spend it. One BTC is one BTC and can never be more or less. This was a problem that had never before been solved in the digital world.

Satoshi's solution was to create a public ledger (called a "blockchain") that would record every single bitcoin transaction. This ledger is stored on every computer running the bitcoin software, and it is secured by another network of computers that are rewarded for their work with newly generated bitcoin. Anyone can see every bitcoin transaction on the blockchain, and because of this, no one can double-spend any bitcoin, alter a previous transaction, or create a new fraudulent transaction. Over time, the network of computers securing the bitcoin blockchain has become the most powerful network of computers in the world.

The public blockchain allowed for the second genius aspect of bitcoin: a solution to the trust issue. Double-spending isn't a problem with a centralized service because every transaction flows through its servers to confirm nothing is being spent twice (this is essentially how digital fiat-money transactions are done). But the trade-off is that every user must completely trust the service and those who run it. Satoshi recognized that centralized services rob money of its independence. So he created bitcoin to be a trustless, decentralized protocol.

A trustless system also increases the verifiability of the money it uses. Remember, for a good to be strong money, one must be able to verify that his money is actually what it claims to be. When it comes to natural goods, like gold or coconuts, natural methods can verify authenticity. For paper or digital fiat money, the verifiability moves to a trusted third party: Is the piece of paper or number on your account really what it says it is? A bank or credit card company is needed to confirm that yes, this really is acceptable money.

In fact, with digital transactions, as many as six or seven other trusted third parties may be involved in securing and verifying the transaction as it moves along the internet (with each party taking a small fee off the transaction). At any point one of those third parties could break trust and manipulate the transaction in its favor.

For the user, all this happens behind the scenes. A Venmo user enters his bank or credit card information, and then "instantly" sends money to another user. But before Venmo truly sends the funds, it needs to verify many things. First, that the user has the money in his account. Then, a series of payment processors verify the transaction while sending that payment to the recipient's bank, which also needs to confirm it is legitimate. This process involves the sender's bank, Venmo, various credit card companies and payment processors, and the receiver's bank. Everyone in this process must verify that yes, this customer has the money he claims to be able to spend. They also must all be trusted to handle the funds along the way.

Bitcoin eliminates all these trusted third parties and allows someone to send money directly from person to person over the internet. Using bitcoin breaks one's dependence on third parties to verify transactions.

Notice how Satoshi originally called bitcoin an electronic *cash* system. He used the analogy of cash to show that an online bitcoin transaction is much like a real-world cash transaction. When I give cash to the little girl running the neighborhood lemonade stand, neither of us needs to trust each other or any third party. The cash itself is verifiable.[34] Bitcoin works like that: one person transfers money to another person without needing to trust any third party or even the other person in the transaction.

COMMON QUESTIONS

This basic explanation usually leads to a few important questions, such as, What exactly *is* bitcoin? I can't see it or touch it or hold it, so what is it?

---

[34] This assumes no counterfeiting of the cash, which isn't much of a problem in real life anymore. We'll see that bitcoin cannot be counterfeited.

Essentially bitcoin is simply digital information, just like anything that resides on computers and the internet. Although there are many images of bitcoin "coins" in news stories about bitcoin, there are no physical bitcoin coins. It's 100 percent digital.

This leads to another question: If bitcoin is just zeros and ones stored on computers, why is bitcoin worth anything?

Let's recall what made any good used as money "worth" something historically. It was because that good ranked highly in the seven monetary properties—higher than other alternatives. Yes, gold can be used for something other than money (just like feathers and coconuts and seashells can be), but that's not what makes it worthwhile as money. After all, other metals like copper can also be useful (and may be more useful than gold in many ways), but they were rarely accepted as money because they didn't rank highly for monetary properties.

Bitcoin, as we'll see, ranks highly in those seven properties; in fact, its overall ranking is better than any other good used as money in history.

A final question that also inevitably arises is, Who controls the bitcoin network? This is like asking who controls email, or who controls the internet. A country can try to ban certain websites, but there's always a way around those bans—the country does not truly control the internet. No one entity, or even group of entities, controls any of these things, and no one controls the bitcoin network. In fact, Satoshi Nakamoto himself, if he were to return to the public eye, would have no more control over bitcoin than anyone else.

Bitcoin, like email and the internet, is run by a protocol, or a set of rules determined by software. This software is open to the public for anyone to see (this type of software is known as "open-source software"), so anyone who wants to can see what its governing rules are. A group of programmers maintain the software, but they don't control it.

For any change these developers want to make, they need consensus; specifically, they need the thousands of people running the bitcoin software to agree to upgrade the software with the proposed changes. No one person or organization can force a change to the protocol software; it must be accepted by the many bitcoin operators spread throughout the world. Does this sound like an elite group? Note that anyone can easily become one of these operators—all it takes is a halfway decent computer and an internet connection. Consensus among all these thousands of diverse operators is needed in order to make even the most minor change to the protocol.

BEYOND THE BASICS

Now that I've given a basic overview of how bitcoin works, we're ready for more. While some of these details might be confusing initially, understanding them even on a basic level will help us discover why bitcoin is the most moral money ever created. So let's dig in.

Bitcoin is a decentralized global monetary system consisting of both an electronic payment network and the digital money used on that network.[35] In today's world, payment

---

[35] In the early years of bitcoin, the payment network was called "Bitcoin" (with the *B* capitalized) and the money was referred to as "bitcoins" (plural and not capitalized). However, in recent years most people just refer to both as "bitcoin" (with both meanings lowercased), even when referring to more than one bitcoin ("I own two bitcoin.").

networks and money are usually separate; for example, dollars, euros, and yen are all *forms of money*, and credit cards make up *payment networks* that allow you to spend those forms of money more easily. However, with bitcoin the network and money combine into one integrated system. In this book we're mostly interested in evaluating bitcoin as a form of money, but without the underlying payment network, it couldn't actually be used as money; that is, it wouldn't be useful and efficient and rank highly in the monetary properties such as portability and fungibility (How portable, for example, is a money you can't spend anywhere?).

When bitcoin was first introduced to the world, its few supporters thought of it primarily as a payment system (thus the title of the bitcoin white paper: "Bitcoin: A Peer-to-Peer Electronic Cash System"). The emphasis of many bitcoiners in the first few years was the desire to replace our faulty modern system of credit cards and other payment systems with something better. But sitting in the background was always another important aspect of bitcoin, one that Satoshi baked into its design: bitcoin as not just a new payment system but a whole new form of money.

THE BLOCKCHAIN

The foundation of the bitcoin payment network is the blockchain, the public ledger of all bitcoin transactions. The bitcoin payment network is called the blockchain because all transactions are grouped in "blocks" that are "chained" together all the way back to the first block ever created.

Every time someone transfers bitcoin to another person, the transaction is transmitted to the bitcoin network. The bitcoin network then groups together the most recent transactions (prioritizing the transactions that paid the highest fees) in one block. When this new block is added to the blockchain, the new transaction is included and is thus recorded on the bitcoin network.

For example, if Alice sends 0.03 BTC to Bob at 10:59 a.m. on September 9, 2024, that transaction is permanently recorded on the blockchain, which lets the whole network know that Alice controls 0.03 less BTC and that Bob controls 0.03 more. The blockchain does not record the identities of Alice and Bob; it just records the bitcoin addresses involved in the transaction—bitcoin addresses that Alice and Bob control. Bitcoin transactions are thus **pseudonymous**. We'll explain this aspect of bitcoin more in a moment.

BITCOIN NODES

The bitcoin blockchain is stored on every computer in the world that is running a full "node" on the bitcoin network. There's no centralized blockchain that each node coordinates with; instead, each node holds the entire blockchain independently, and then through the rules of the bitcoin protocol software, each node checks with every other node to confirm the validity of its copy and every other copy.

Anyone can run a bitcoin node; all it takes is an average computer and an internet connection. The bitcoin protocol software is free to download. The ease of running a node—which means many people around the world do run a node—makes the bitcoin network difficult to attack. Even if someone could shut down all the nodes in a single country (which itself would be incredibly difficult), nodes would still be running elsewhere around the globe. As of this writing, there are more than twenty thousand nodes operating throughout the world.

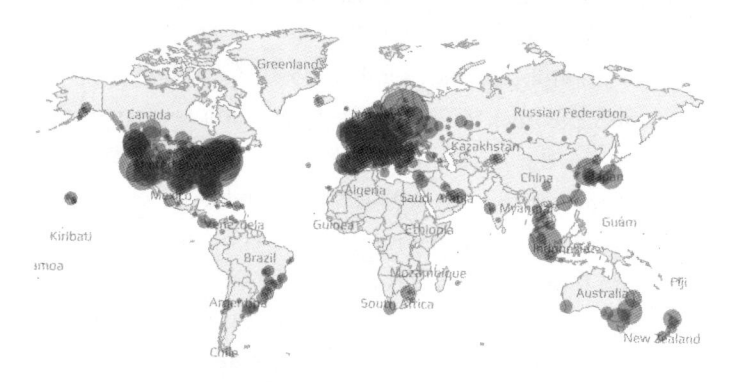

As of December 23, 2024, bitcoin nodes are running in ninety-five countries on six continents (source: Yeow, A. (March 21, 2025). Bitnodes Project. Retrieved from https://bitnodes.io).

The fact that bitcoin nodes run independently and everywhere is what makes bitcoin decentralized; and it prevents any one person or organization from taking control of the bitcoin network. A centralized command center would be vulnerable to attack, so there isn't one.[36]

To update the bitcoin protocol by changing the software, the node operators must agree to upgrade their software with the proposed changes. A programmer might propose a change

[36] This decentralized design finds its origins in the internet itself, which was initially created by the U.S. military during the Cold War to remain in operation even in the case of a nuclear war. The internet would be a decentralized network without a single point of failure and no one entity controlling it. Eventually the U.S. government found it couldn't control the internet either.

he believes will improve bitcoin substantially, but if the node operators don't accept that change, then the protocol remains unchanged. The changes that the majority of the node operators do accept become part of the protocol.

BITCOIN MINING

A block is added to the blockchain by a process called "mining." Mining is done by another class of computers on the bitcoin network: miners. In theory, anyone can be a miner, just like anyone can be a node operator, but mining computers are far more expensive to purchase and maintain (we'll see why in a moment). Whereas nodes maintain the integrity of the blockchain by verifying its accuracy, miners secure the network and add new blocks to the blockchain.

The mining process consists of many computers in a contest to see which can solve a complex mathematical challenge first. The winner gets to officially add the new block to the blockchain and is rewarded for his effort with newly created bitcoin.

Before I explain how mining works and why it involves a mathematical challenge, we should pause for a moment here. What do I mean by "newly created bitcoin"? When the bitcoin network was initially launched, it had exactly one block (the "Genesis Block"), which generated fifty new bitcoin.[37] Why didn't Satoshi just include the entire money supply of BTC in the initial launch of the network? Because he wanted

---

[37] Due to the unique nature of the Genesis Block, the fifty bitcoin in that block are not controlled by anyone (not even Satoshi) and cannot be spent.

to mimic the process by which the soundest money before bitcoin—gold—was added to a money supply.

The creation of new bitcoin was to follow a specific, expensive, and time-consuming process, one that diametrically opposes the process for creating fiat money (which is essentially someone in a country's central bank saying, "Let there be more money!" and pressing a button on a computer keyboard).

When bitcoin was first introduced, each block generated fifty new bitcoin—the "block reward." In other words, whoever mined a new block would receive a balance of fifty BTC in his BTC wallet. Because bitcoin itself was new, these new BTC were essentially worthless, as few people gave them value. However, Satoshi's hope in 2009 and 2010 (which was realized) was that some people would recognize bitcoin's potential and mine BTC, believing it would increase in value over time. At the time of this writing, a single bitcoin is worth around $100,000, so those blocks of fifty BTC created in 2009 are now worth $5 million each.

So far, this monetary policy doesn't seem too different from fiat, if only more regular and time-consuming. A monetary system that creates over seven thousand new units a day is by definition quite inflationary. In hard forms of money, such as gold, it's difficult to add new supply to the existing supply of money, and typically a very small amount is added each year in comparison to the overall existing supply.[38]

---

[38] This is called a money's "stock-to-flow" ratio: how much new money flows into a money supply in comparison to how much supply already exists. For precious metals, this ratio is large (which is good); for fiat money, it can become quite small depending on how much new money a government is creating.

Satoshi wanted bitcoin to eventually have a similar low emission rate, so he designed a mechanism to gradually decrease the number of new BTC created with each block.

Every four years or so,[39] the block reward is cut in half, which is called a "halving." In 2012, the block reward dropped to 25 BTC; in 2016, it dropped to 12.5 BTC. Here is a list of all the previous halvings and the next scheduled one:

November 28, 2012: 25 BTC
July 9, 2016: 12.5 BTC
May 11, 2020: 6.25 BTC
April 19, 2024: 3.125 BTC
Mid-2028: 1.5625 BTC

So, while bitcoin continues to be inflationary (new money is still being created), the rate of inflation steadily decreases, and on a schedule that anyone can follow. There are no surprise injections of new money, as happens in a fiat system, nor new previously unknown deposits of money found, as with precious metals. This process of decreasing inflation continues until no more new BTC is created when a new block is added to the blockchain. At that point, bitcoin inflation stops completely.[40]

---

[39] Actually, every 210,000 blocks. The bitcoin network does not have an internal clock, nor does it access an external clock, so it measures everything in the number of blocks created instead of seconds or minutes or other standard units of time.

[40] Fees for transactions are also added to the block reward, which is BTC paid by the sender of the BTC. So the block reward is new BTC plus all transaction fees of that block. Eventually, when no new BTC are generated (around the year 2140), then the entire block reward will consist only of transaction fees.

This is scheduled to occur around A.D. 2140, and at that time there will be a total of twenty-one million BTC.

This schedule means the vast majority of bitcoin is created in its early years. Even though there are another one hundred–plus years of block rewards, as of this writing, already more than nineteen million BTC of the twenty-one million total have been created. An easy way to remember this schedule is the following:

> In the first epoch, fifty BTC are created every block, and during this epoch 50 percent of all BTC are created and 50 percent remain to be created.

> In the second epoch, twenty-five BTC are created every block, and during this epoch 25 percent of all BTC are created and 25 percent remain to be created.

> In the third epoch, 12.5 BTC are created every block, and during this epoch 12.5 percent of all BTC are created and 12.5 percent remain to be created.

> And so on.

So you can see that, as we are now in the epoch which creates 3.125 BTC per block, the vast majority of all BTC has been created.

This staggered inflation rate, and the total cap of twenty-one million BTC, has become one of the most enshrined aspects of bitcoin. In theory, someone could propose to change the rate and the total cap in the protocol. Modifying the software in this way would not be technically difficult. However, the likelihood that the bitcoin node operators would accept this change is essentially nil. Bitcoiners debate about many things, but the twenty-one million BTC money supply is accepted as fixed by all.

Now back to the actual bitcoin mining process.

Bitcoin mining is centered around computers in a competition to be the first to solve a mathematical challenge. This might sound silly at first, but bear with me — I'll explain why it's like this in a moment. This mathematical challenge is analogous to a game of dice. Imagine fifty people, each with a pair of one-thousand-sided dice: one hundred dice in total. Each person gets to roll his dice as quickly as he can, and the first person to roll a sum under ten wins the game.

In this example, everyone has essentially the same chance of winning, and it's luck that determines who rolls under ten first. If there are fewer contestants, then the odds of each person winning increases, but the average time for someone to roll under ten will also increase. If we add contestants, then the odds of winning go down, as does the average time until someone wins.

Now let's say someone obtains ten more thousand-sided dice and begins to roll them as well. He now has twelve dice he rolls each time. This gives him a better chance of winning than before, but his victory is not guaranteed, because another contestant could roll under ten at any time.

This is essentially how bitcoin mining works. Computers compete with each other to see who wins the challenge first, completing a mathematical computation in order to guess a particular value. Because it is a race to see who is lucky enough to come up with the appropriate value, the faster a computer can "roll the dice," the more likely it is that it will win. When bitcoin was first introduced, regular desktop computers competed in this process, but now specifically configured and highly powered computers are made just to mine the fastest. This is analogous to having more and more thousand-sided dice to roll.

It might seem at first that this is a nonsensical process, but we know that Satoshi intentionally created bitcoin to mimic a core characteristic of gold in creating new bitcoin: work is required for mining. New money should not be easily created. It takes energy and work in order to be rewarded new bitcoin; a money that was easily created would not be valued.

Although fiat money can be digital, as is bitcoin, its creation is fundamentally different: one requires work; one does not. This concept is known as "proof of work": in order to mine new bitcoin, you have to prove you are willing to spend time and energy to do so. It's the opposite of a small group of powerful government officials simply creating new money by fiat. Bitcoin is scarce; fiats are not.

Most importantly, the process of mining makes bitcoin incredibly secure. Remember, mining not only generates new bitcoin, but it also adds transactions to the public ledger known as the blockchain. Because it takes so much processing power to mine a block and thus confirm a transaction, the resources that would be needed to take over the bitcoin mining network and control the transactions are astronomical.[41]

[41] There is a theoretical attack vector against bitcoin called a "51 percent attack," in which a single entity controls more than 50 percent of all bitcoin mining, and in theory, would then be able to manipulate the transactions in a new block to its benefit. This has never occurred in bitcoin's history, and now the processing power

Furthermore, past blocks become more secure over time. Each block contains many transactions, and each block is connected to the chain of previous blocks. The longer a block has been on the blockchain, the more secure it is. This is because each block added confirms the validity of all the blocks before it; when a new block is confirmed by a miner, the miner is also confirming every block that came before it.

Imagine someone stacking thousand-pound weights, one on top of the other. It would be incredibly difficult to lift the top weight off the stack. But imagine if the stack contained five hundred weights, and you had to lift the top three hundred! The computer processing power it would take to hack and manipulate a transaction that's in a block just a few days old is more than all the processing power that exists in the world. The bitcoin mining process has created the most secure network on earth.

The bitcoin protocol is designed so that it will take, on average, ten minutes to solve the next mathematical challenge and mine a block. As the value of bitcoin has increased, the number of people mining bitcoin has also increased, and this has created an arms race of sorts to build faster, more powerful computers that can solve the mathematical challenge more quickly and thus be rewarded more often. Millions of dollars are spent each year mining bitcoin, and those thousands of powerful computers continually mining are securing the network, all in hopes of being rewarded with more bitcoin.

Satoshi anticipated this mining arms race, and so he included a **difficulty adjustment** in the bitcoin protocol. As we

---

behind bitcoin is so vast that it would be practically impossible to achieve.

noted, mining occurs by computers racing to be the first to solve mathematical challenges. Remember our hypothetical dice-rolling situation? Let's further imagine that the dice establishment wants the average time it takes to win—the average length of each contest—to be ten minutes. After a hundred contests, it sees that the average time to roll under ten is actually nine minutes. What does it do? It increases the difficulty by changing the rules: now a contestant has to roll under nine to win. If the average time came out to eleven minutes, it might decrease the difficulty of winning by stating that a contestant must roll under eleven to win. It adjusts the difficulty periodically to make sure the average time remains constant.

The difficulty of the bitcoin-mining mathematical challenge is set so it takes around ten minutes for the first computer to solve it. But what if someone builds a more powerful computer, one dedicated to mining BTC and far more powerful than existing computers? Then it could mine blocks faster than every ten minutes, which increases the real-world inflation rate. Instead of just 144 new blocks confirmed in a day, the miners could confirm dozens more a day.

Satoshi designed bitcoin so that every 2,016 blocks (which comes out to every fourteen days at ten minutes per block), the protocol looks back at how quickly blocks were created and adjusts the difficulty of the mathematical challenges to be solved. If blocks were created more quickly than every ten minutes, then the difficulty is increased to slow down the process; if for some reason blocks were created less quickly than every ten minutes, then the difficulty is decreased. This process ensures a reliable and steady inflation rate over time. It also means that bitcoin is designed to be

scarce—an advancement in mining computer technology cannot result in the market being flooded with new BTC.

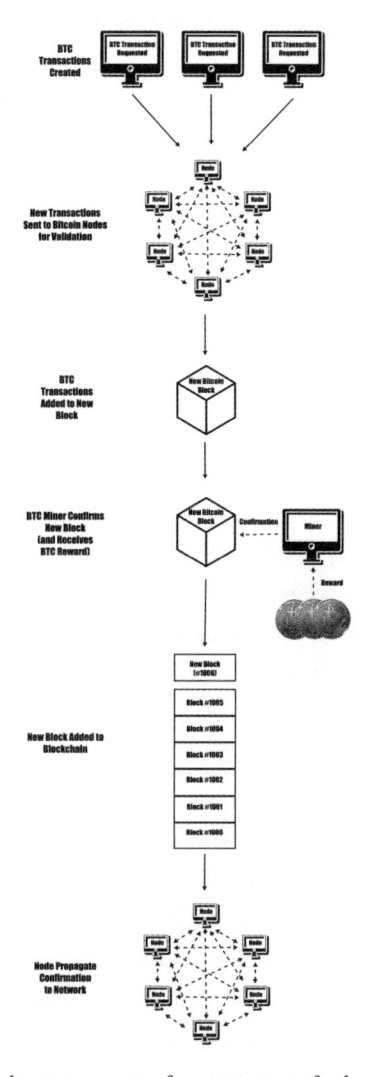

The life of a bitcoin transaction from initiation to final confirmation.

BITCOIN USERS

Now we need to move from nodes and miners to users of bitcoin. After all, this is what matters: How does a person hold and use bitcoin? Like other aspects of bitcoin, the answer is a bit complicated, for one doesn't actually "hold" bitcoin like she might hold dollar bills in her physical wallet. No bitcoin ever resides on a person's computer like an image or document does. This is due to Satoshi's solution to the "double-spend" problem we mentioned earlier—if bitcoins are just files on your computer, you can copy and send them over and over again. Instead, what a bitcoin user *does* hold is the **private key** to control specified amounts of bitcoin on the network.

Let's return for a moment to our email analogy. To send someone an email, you need his email address. That email address is public—if people didn't know it, no one could send someone an email. But the ability to *access* that email is private; in other words, a password is needed. There are two parts, then, to sending and receiving email: a public aspect (an email address) and a private one (the password). Bitcoin works in a similar fashion: it consists of public addresses and private keys.

Here's where the analogy with email breaks down, however. When someone sends you an email, a file containing the contents of that email resides on your computer. Or perhaps it's on your internet provider's server. The important point is that it's a file on one specific computer. Bitcoin, conversely, does not store a file for each and every bitcoin on the network; instead, it records on the blockchain the *balances* of each bitcoin address—there are no digital coin files, just a ledger that notes the amounts of bitcoin sent and received to and from various bitcoin addresses.

Another difference between email and bitcoin is that bitcoin balances are not simply protected by passwords, which are notoriously easy to crack. Passwords must be stored on a central database. Since the entire point of bitcoin is to liberate money from centralized systems which have all the weaknesses discussed in chapters 3 and 4, passwords are not used to protect a person's bitcoin balances.

Instead, bitcoin employs a process known as public-key encryption. This, by the way, is where we get the generic term for bitcoin, "cryptocurrency" — a currency based on cryptography rather than backed by governments or provided by nature. The public address and the private key are actually mathematically related to one another, and due to a bit of mathematical magic behind public-key encryption, the private key is the only way to "unlock" access to the bitcoin balance controlled by that public address.

To understand public-key encryption, let's compare it to the following scenario. I tell you that I wrote a mathematical equation on a piece of paper and I want you to guess the equation. I also tell you that the answer to the equation is the number 7. Can you guess the equation? It's highly unlikely: it could be 10-3 or 210÷30 or ([5*3]+20)÷5 or 10,000-9,993. There's no way to know what I wrote down; it could take centuries for you to guess correctly.

I could make it easier by reducing the data set; I could tell you that the equation only contains integers less than 100 and is either an addition or subtraction equation. Now it's possible to guess my equation in a reasonable time frame. The larger the data set, the harder it is to solve; the smaller the data set, the easier.

Here's the trick: while it's incredibly difficult to guess the equation, it's incredibly easy to verify that the answer is correct: yes, ten minus three does equal seven. In one direction the challenge is hard; in the other direction it is easy. That's what happens with public-key encryption: it's effectively impossible to know a private key based on the public address, but it's very easy to verify that an address was properly accessed by a private key. In the case of bitcoin, the encryption used on transactions would take the computers of today so long to break that the universe would experience heat death before they succeeded—the data set is that large.[42] But it's trivial to confirm that a properly decrypted transaction (by the appropriate private key) is valid.

Bitcoin users use software "wallets" that automatically take care of the management of public addresses and private keys and how they are used to send and receive transactions. A bitcoin wallet—which can be a program on a computer, an app on a smart phone, or even a dedicated hardware device—holds the addresses and private keys and so can unlock any BTC under the user's control.

A bitcoin public address can control any balance of bitcoin, whether it be 1,000 BTC, or 1 BTC, or 0.0001 BTC, and a wallet can hold thousands of addresses. Bitcoin is divisible up to eight decimal places. So the smallest denomination of bitcoin is 0.00000001, which is called a "satoshi," or "sat," after bitcoin's founder. But since the number of decimal places is programmatically instituted, more places could be added in the future if needed (which, it is important to note, does *not*

---

[42] I'll address the potential danger of quantum computers breaking bitcoin's encryption in Chapter 8, "Objections to Bitcoin."

increase the overall supply of money—cutting a pizza into more slices does not create more pizza). Bitcoin is theoretically infinitely divisible.

We're going to look under the hood now, so don't be alarmed if the process of exactly how the bitcoin network handles sending and receiving bitcoin seems confusing. Most wallets hide this confusion and keep things simple for the user. Here are the basics of what happens underneath.

Let's say Alice wants to send 0.05 BTC to Bob. She currently has a balance of 1 BTC in her wallet, all at one address (again, remember that 1 BTC doesn't reside in a file in her wallet software, but instead the balance of 1 BTC is recorded on the blockchain ledger for her address). When she tells her wallet to send that 0.05 BTC, the wallet first completely drains her address of the 1 BTC. But don't worry! She won't lose all that BTC. The wallet then divides the 1 BTC into two chunks—one containing 0.05 BTC and the other containing the remaining 0.95 BTC. The 0.05 BTC is sent to the address under Bob's control, and the remaining balance of 0.95 BTC is sent back to another address under the control of Alice's wallet.[43] Alice only sees that she now has a 0.95 BTC balance in her wallet, but under the hood the entire 1 BTC was moved out of the original address.

This process gets more complicated when Alice wants to send BTC from multiple addresses under her control. Let's say that Alice now has 1 BTC in her wallet, but that 1 BTC was

---

[43] Also note that a small transaction fee is taken out to pay the miner who mined the block that contains this transaction. This fee is in addition to the newly created bitcoin the miner also received. So Alice would actually receive back a little less than 0.95 BTC.

previously received in two transactions of 0.5 BTC each to two separate addresses in her wallet (remember, wallets control lots of addresses). She wants to send 0.7 BTC to Catherine. When she hits send, the wallet software takes 0.5 BTC from each address and combines it into a single transaction that sends 0.7 BTC to Catherine, and then sends the remaining 0.3 BTC back to a third address in Alice's wallet.

Again, note that the address management is taken care of by the wallet software automatically; Alice doesn't have to understand it or even know it's happening.

BITCOIN INCENTIVES

From a programming standpoint, bitcoin is one of the best-designed systems ever created. But that's not what truly makes it "work." Satoshi was a skilled programmer, but he was an even better economist. He didn't set out to build an internet-based protocol like email; he was building a new form of money, *which necessitated an understanding of how and why people make the choices they do in their daily lives.* He knew that the design of bitcoin needed to be such that all incentives among all the actors in the bitcoin play—developers, node operators, miners, and users—were aligned. The protocol had to be set up so that each of these groups would all work to keep bitcoin going; however, recognizing the realities of human nature, Satoshi realized that what was best for bitcoin needed to be in their self-interest as well.

It's not just luck, then, that bitcoin has been so successful. Since bitcoin is not a company, it doesn't have a CEO guiding it, nor a marketing department promoting it. Instead, each bitcoin actor, following his own self-interest, ends up guiding and promoting bitcoin as part of a whole, usually without even realizing it. This symphony of action solidifies bitcoin functionally and economically.

The instance of the only software flaw in bitcoin's history is a case study in how these incentives align.

In March 2013—four years after bitcoin's launch and two years after Satoshi left the project—a new version of the bitcoin protocol was released.[44] All bitcoin software releases are **backward compatible**. This means that old versions of the bitcoin software can keep running even after others have updated to the new version. This is also known as a "soft fork." A "hard fork," on the other hand, means the update is not backward compatible. If you don't update your software, you are no longer on the network. Since bitcoin upgrades are soft forks, even if a node operator didn't update his copy of the software, it would still be part of the network.

Typically, when a new version of bitcoin is released, it takes a few months for all the miners and node operators to update their own copies. It's not uncommon for the miners to update first, since mining is a full-time business, whereas node operators are voluntarily running their nodes, so it might not be a top priority for them.

In the case of the March 2013 update—upgrading from version 0.7 to 0.8—a flaw was introduced that actually caused a hard fork.[45] This is a worst-case scenario for bitcoin, because

[44] Like any software, the bitcoin protocol is updated regularly. These software releases typically contain minor changes to increase the efficiency of the network.

[45] Nathaniel Popper, *Digital Gold: Bitcoin and the Inside Story of the Misfits and Millionaires Trying to Reinvent Money* (Harper, 2015), 192–195.

it creates two incompatible blockchains: computers running version 0.7 went off on one chain, while version 0.8 created a new one. Which one was the "true" bitcoin blockchain?

Very quickly the bitcoin community noticed, and everyone realized it was a big deal. As usually happens, most miners, including all the biggest ones, had upgraded to 0.8, and they were confirming blocks — and receiving bitcoin — on that chain. Meanwhile, a small number of miners and most of the node operators were on the 0.7 chain, and it too was producing new blocks, and new bitcoin. Two bitcoin blockchains running concurrently destroys the entire value proposition of bitcoin. How does a user know if the bitcoin he's using is accepted by a bitcoin merchant? When buying bitcoin, which version are you getting? What if another hard fork occurs, causing a third version of bitcoin? This was an existential crisis for bitcoin.

With no CEO to declare the path forward, how could this be resolved? The bitcoin community would need to work via consensus to resolve the problem. This was the greatest test in bitcoin's history of its built-in incentives. Would everyone work together for the good of bitcoin?

If the 0.8 miners downgraded to 0.7, they would lose the hundreds of new bitcoin they had been rewarded in the hours since the hard fork was introduced (each block was generating 25 BTC each at this time). But if the 0.8 chain was declared the "true" blockchain, most of the node operators and some of the smaller miners, who didn't necessarily keep up with the day-to-day goings-on of bitcoin, wouldn't hear about it for weeks or even months. They would continue to run the 0.7 chain during that time, resulting in two competing "bitcoins."

The lead bitcoin developer at the time, Gavin Andresen, suggested that the 0.8 chain be declared the true chain, since it was the one the most powerful actors in the bitcoin community—the miners confirming the vast majority of the blocks—had chosen. It was a reasonable idea, and Andresen was the most influential member of the community at the time. Many bitcoiners saw him as the successor to Satoshi.

However, pushback came immediately from others in the bitcoin community. Yes, these big miners were powerful, but they also could more easily update their software (in this case, downgrading it). It would be far easier to get them to downgrade than to get the eclectic group of node operators and small miners around the world to upgrade. But this course would mean those powerful miners would lose the new bitcoin they had been rewarded since the hard fork, which even then was worth tens of thousands of dollars. And remember, these miners were spending a lot of money to run their servers.

Perhaps surprisingly, the powerful miners immediately agreed that they should downgrade, going against the recommendation of lead developer Andresen. They recognized that their short-term loss of the new bitcoin they'd earned was far less significant than the downfall of the whole network. So it actually wasn't surprising they took this loss, since the structure of bitcoin incentivized them to make the sacrifice for the greater good of bitcoin. When the choice is between losing a few hundred bitcoin or potentially destroying bitcoin, it's not much of a choice after all.

Again, this is the only flaw of this nature ever introduced into the bitcoin software, and within hours the problem was resolved. Not because a strong CEO stepped in and took charge of the situation, but because all the actors in the bitcoin space were incentivized to work for the overall good of the network. Just like Satoshi designed it.

Now that we have seen how bitcoin works both technically and economically, we need to explore how bitcoin's design makes it the most useful and the most moral money ever created.

Chapter 6

The Properties of Bitcoin

> *As a thought experiment, imagine there was a base metal as scarce as gold but with the following properties: boring grey in colour; not a good conductor of electricity; not particularly strong, but not ductile or easily malleable either; not useful for any practical or ornamental purpose — and one special, magical property: can be transported over a communications channel.*

—Satoshi Nakamoto[46]

[46] Posted at Bitcoin Forum, August 27, 2010, punctuation adapted, https://bitcointalk.org/index.php?topic=583.msg11405#msg11405.

IN CHAPTER 2 we studied what makes good money, in terms of both usefulness and morality. By evaluating a form of money according to the seven properties of money — divisibility, portability, durability, fungibility, verifiability, scarcity, and independence — we can rank each form. We'll use these properties to evaluate bitcoin, but first, for comparison's sake we can look at this chart (on page 110) ranking the seven properties of various historical forms of money.

Fiat money and precious metals all rank as highly useful, but fiat receives a low moral ranking, while copper, silver, and gold are the most moral. Let us now turn to bitcoin to judge how it ranks in comparison.

BITCOIN'S USEFULNESS AND EFFICIENCY

The primary focus of this book on the morality of the bitcoin monetary system does not mean we shouldn't consider bitcoin's usefulness and efficiency. No matter how moral a money might be in theory, if it can't actually be used in the real world, it's not really money.

First, bitcoin is highly **divisible**. As noted in the previous chapter, a single bitcoin can be divided to the eighth decimal place, all the way down to a single satoshi. No previous form of money, not even the dollar, is as divisible as bitcoin. Further, since bitcoin is programmable money, it can be divided even further in the future if necessary.

PROPERTY RANKING OF VARIOUS FORMS OF MONEY

	USEFULNESS					MORALITY			
	DIVISIBLE	PORTABLE	DURABLE	FUNGIBLE	OVERALL USE	VERIFIABLE	SCARCE	INDEPENDENT	OVERALL MORALITY
FEATHERS	low	above average	low	low	low	fair	low	above average	fair
TEETH	low	above average	low	low	low	fair	low	above average	fair
SEASHELLS	low	above average	low	fair	fair	fair	low	above average	fair
STONES	low	fair	high	low	fair	fair	low	high	fair
COPPER	above average	fair	above average	high	above average	above average	fair	high	above average
SILVER	above average	fair	high	high	high	above average	above average	high	above average
GOLD	fair	fair	high	high	high	above average	above average	high	above average
FIAT	high	high	fair	high	high	fair	low	low	low

Next, bitcoin is incredibly **portable**. A person can store the keys that access any amount of bitcoin on a computer, a smartphone, or a small hardware device. She can also move that bitcoin around the world almost instantaneously. In fact, bitcoin is the most portable money ever created. Consider trying to transport a billion dollars in three different forms of money: gold, U.S. dollars, and bitcoin. To move that much gold involves significant resources in both security and transportation. To move a billion dollars denominated in paper bills would also be difficult, although nowhere near as difficult as gold. Sending one billion dollars in digital form would be far easier, but the transaction would need significant verifications (and approval) from third parties like banks and other financial institutions, each of which would charge sizable fees and would likely raise many questions about the transaction. Sending a billion dollars in bitcoin across the world? It would take just a few minutes and cost only a few dollars.[47]

Bitcoin's portability extends even further. One aspect of monetary portability is the ability to travel while carrying a specific form of money. Imagine a person trying to flee an oppressive government and settle in a new land. If his money is in gold, it's likely he won't be able to bring much with him, and what he does bring could easily be confiscated by border patrols. Fiat money stored in a bank account would likely be seized, as would any fiat money held in paper form while crossing a border. Bitcoin, however, can be transported without out a person having to carry any physical money or device.

Most bitcoin wallets use a set of words that, when entered in the correct order, allow one to recreate the wallet elsewhere

---

[47] At current bitcoin transaction rates.

and access all the bitcoin controlled by that wallet. Called a "seed phrase," this set of words acts as a backup in case a wallet is lost or destroyed.[48] If a person memorizes this set of words, all his bitcoin is available to him anywhere in the world if he simply enters those words into a new wallet. Never before has money been this portable.

When it comes to **durability**, it's harder to judge bitcoin, since it's so different from previous forms of money. Gold is very difficult to destroy, whereas destroying paper is easy. A digital asset is a mixture: both highly durable and susceptible to easy destruction. It is highly durable in that although a single wallet device may be destroyed, if a person knows his seed phrase, he can still access his bitcoin. A copy of this phrase on a piece of paper or engraved on a piece of metal allows continued access to bitcoin even in the event of a wallet's destruction. However, a digital asset like bitcoin can be easily lost forever in other ways. If a person loses his wallet and his backup seed phrase or doesn't use proper security procedures related to his wallet, all his bitcoin funds could be lost. Bitcoin itself is very durable, but it can be lost due to user error.

Finally, with regard to usefulness, bitcoin is **fungible**. One BTC always equals one BTC. The bitcoin blockchain securely tracks all bitcoin balances, and no balance is favored over any others or worth more than any others. Since bitcoin is decentralized, no central entity can mark out any bitcoin balance in any special way.

---

[48] A seed phrase is a random set of typically twelve, twenty, or twenty-four words that acts as a backup for someone's bitcoin wallet. It can be used to create a new instance of that wallet on another device. We'll discuss seed phrases in more detail in chapter 10, "Getting Started with Bitcoin."

We can see from this brief overview that bitcoin is highly useful and efficient as a form of money—far more useful and efficient than precious metals and other historical forms of money. It is also at least as useful and efficient as fiat money.

BITCOIN'S MORAL PROPERTIES

How does bitcoin rank in terms of the moral properties of money?

Bitcoin is exceptionally **verifiable**. Due to the open-source nature of the software protocol, the cryptography used to secure transactions, and the mining process that confirms all transactions, every bitcoin transaction can be verified as legitimate within minutes of being sent to the network. Verification, in fact, is a core process for every bitcoin transaction; if a transaction is in any way fraudulent, it is quickly discarded and not added to the blockchain. Further, anyone can verify a bitcoin transaction as legitimate simply by checking to see if it's confirmed on the public blockchain. Compare this to fiat money, in which a trusted third party is required to verify every non-cash transaction, a process that can take days or even months in some cases.

When it comes to **scarcity**, bitcoin outclasses all forms of money. Never before has there been a fixed upper limit to a money's supply. Government officials can create fiat money out of thin air; increases to the money supply of forms of money based on nature, such as gold, are more difficult but still possible. Although new gold is costly to mine, new deposits are still being found each year. In the future, gold could even be mined in space, where it is thought to be abundant. But twenty-one million is the limit for bitcoin: there will never be more than that, making it the most scarce form of money in history.

We need to take a moment to pause on this particular monetary property, for it represents the most fundamental difference between bitcoin and all other forms of money. Of all the technological, economic, and moral advances that bitcoin represents, this fixed upper limit of twenty-one million bitcoin is the most important, and the absolute fixed limit sets bitcoin apart as unique among all forms of money. The scarcity of bitcoin is the key property that makes it far more moral than fiat-money systems.

Consider this chart of the M2 money supply from 1959 to the present.[49] M2 is the measure of U.S. dollars in the economy, including cash, checking deposits, and other deposits readily convertible to cash, such as CDs. When the Federal Reserve adds money to the economy, this is where it ends up.

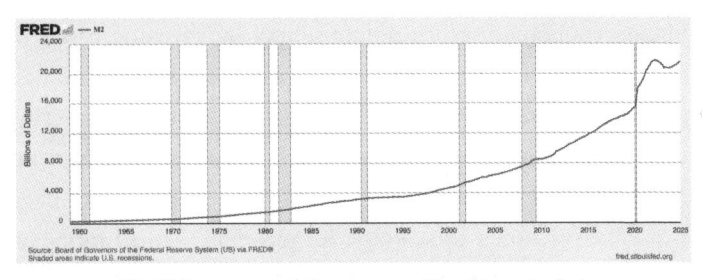

The U.S. money supply has risen steadily, with particularly rapid growth in the twenty-first century.

We see a steady increase in money supply during the 1960s and 1970s, but then the rate of increase begins to rise in

[49]   Source: Board of Governors of the Federal Reserve System (US), M2 [M2SL], retrieved from FRED, Federal Reserve Bank of St. Louis; https://fred.stlouisfed.org/series/M2SL, March 18, 2025.

the 1980s, and by the 2000s it is escalating quite rapidly. In response to the 2008 financial crisis the money supply shot up even more, becoming almost vertical during the 2020 COVID-19 pandemic.

We have no idea what this chart will look like in the future: When another crisis hits, how much more money will be pumped into the economy? When the money supply is not scarce and can be manipulated at will, then inevitably inflation, even rapid inflation, will result. We know that inflation always leads to rising prices, which dramatically impact the lives and life decisions of everyone, but especially the poor and middle class. In 2022, after the massive increase in the money supply following the pandemic, even the underestimating Consumer Price Index (CPI) reached 8 percent, its highest level since 1981.[50]

Even a natural form of money such as gold can have "supply shocks," such as happened in the middle of the nineteenth century when vast deposits of gold were found in California.

While gold is not as susceptible to the extreme yet regular supply increases of fiat money, its inflation rate is not predictable, as this chart of world gold production from 1820 to 1860 shows.[51]

---

[50] "Consumer Price Index, 1913–," Federal Reserve Bank of Minneapolis, https://www.minneapolisfed.org/about-us/monetary-policy/inflation-calculator/consumer-price-index-1913-. The Consumer Price Index measures change over time in the prices paid by consumers for a supposedly representative basket of goods and services.

[51] Source: Our World in Data, https://ourworldindata.org/grapher/gold-production?time=1800..1853.

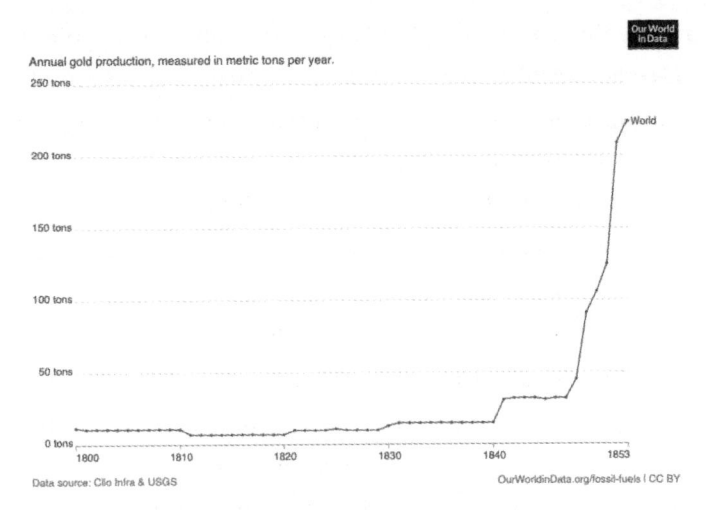

After the California gold rush of the 1850s,
overall worldwide gold supply skyrocketed.

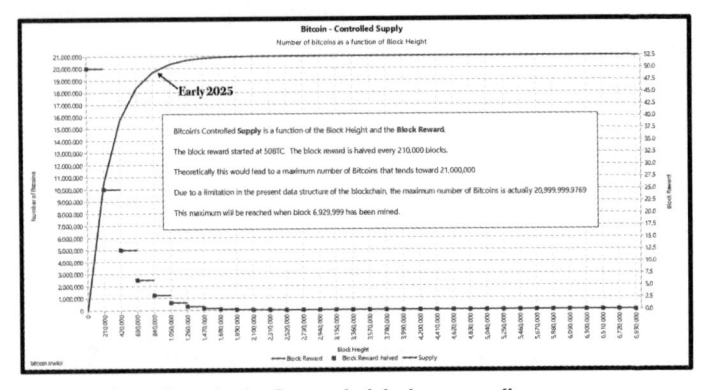

Bitcoin has a fixed inflation schedule that eventually goes to zero.

In contrast, consider this bitcoin supply chart, which also includes the halving cycle.[52] (If you're not sure what "halving" is, refer to chapter 5.)

[52] Source: Bitcoin Wiki, https://en.bitcoin.it/wiki/File:Controlled_supply-supply_over_block_height.png.

We see that the total supply of bitcoin rapidly increased in the early years of the network: fifty new BTC were added every ten minutes, which equals more than 2.6 million per year during the first four years. But every four years the new amount created is halved, so that currently only 3.125 BTC are added every ten minutes. As of late 2024, more than nineteen million of the total twenty-one million BTC have already been created—almost 95 percent of the eventual total. The supply curve (which represents the inflation rate) quickly flattens after the first fifteen years or so, and we can see that within the next decade the inflation rate will become almost zero in comparison to the total money supply. This is an image of the *scarcity* of bitcoin—the money supply is not determined by a small group of Federal Reserve officials or by people trying to find more in nature; it's fixed forever by the bitcoin protocol.

Lastly, bitcoin is **independent**. As I noted when I explained how bitcoin works, it is fundamentally decentralized and controlled by no one, which means no one can manipulate the supply of it, whereas the Federal Reserve controls the U.S. dollar in a highly centralized way. Fiat, which is a creation of the state, is the least independent of all forms of money, but even natural forms of money are at least in theory susceptible to manipulation by powerful forces. For example, since one cannot control where gold mines exist, the governments of countries with large gold deposits could control their output. With bitcoin, if one country bans bitcoin mining, as China did in 2021, bitcoin miners in other countries are unaffected. In fact, in response to China's bitcoin mining ban, mining operations increased in other areas of the world (particularly in Texas), so the overall security of the network was unaffected.

Bitcoin is also independent because it has immediate settlement. *Settlement* refers to the process by which a financial transaction is finalized. In our fiat system, it typically takes up to ninety days before a credit card transaction is truly settled. Before settlement it can be reversed by either party or even by the middlemen involved in the transaction (banks, credit card companies). In 2022, the Canadian government was able to freeze the donations to Canadian truckers protesting COVID-19 restrictions. They could do this because donations sent to the newly formed nonprofit's website had not yet been settled; they were not yet truly owned by the truckers. A bitcoin transaction, on the other hand, settles within minutes and is therefore nonreversible.

Finally, bitcoin is independent because a person can take full ownership of his bitcoin. Digital forms of fiat money can be confiscated by governments and banks because a "trusted" third party actually holds the money. Owning bitcoin, in contrast, means you are your own bank and have complete and total control over your funds.

Bitcoin, then, excels in the moral properties of money, far exceeding fiat and even topping precious metals. Let's return to our chart and add bitcoin to the mix:

Bitcoin, in view of the properties of money, is the best form of money ever. It is both more useful and more moral than the two most common forms of money in history: gold and fiat. The superior moral properties of bitcoin aren't just theoretical properties to be studied in a chart, however; they have far-reaching implications in our society. These strong moral properties incentivize moral behavior over immoral behavior in both institutions and individuals. We'll explore why in the next chapter.

PROPERTY RANKING OF VARIOUS FORMS OF MONEY

| | USEFULNESS | | | | | MORALITY | | | |
	DIVISIBLE	PORTABLE	DURABLE	FUNGIBLE	OVERALL USE	VERIFIABLE	SCARCE	INDEPENDENT	OVERALL MORALITY
FEATHERS	low	above average	low	low	low	fair	low	above average	fair
TEETH	low	above average	low	low	low	fair	low	above average	fair
SEASHELLS	low	above average	low	fair	fair	fair	low	above average	fair
STONES	low	fair	high	low	fair	fair	low	high	fair
COPPER	above average	fair	above average	high	above average	above average	fair	high	above average
SILVER	above average	fair	high	high	high	above average	above average	high	above average
GOLD	fair	fair	high	high	high	above average	above average	high	above average
FIAT	high	high	fair	high	high	fair	low	low	low
BITCOIN	high	high	above average	high	high	high	high	high	high

Chapter 7

Why Bitcoin Is Moral Money

Bitcoin aligns with Natural Law.

—Jimmy Song, author, *Thank God for Bitcoin*[53]

53 Jimmy Song, "The Moral Case for Bitcoin," The Bitcoin Times, December 26, 2020, https://medium.com/the-bitcoin-times/the-moral-case-for-bitcoin-561ed592a464.

BITCOIN'S DESIGN MEANS it ranks highly in the moral properties of money, but so far this might just sound theoretical. Money itself is a tool and therefore doesn't make moral choices; it's what individuals who use money do that matters. However, since different forms of money push individuals and institutions toward more moral or less moral decisions, we need to examine the tool closely. How exactly does bitcoin's design impact our moral choices? That's what we'll explore now.

The most important characteristic of bitcoin's design from a moral standpoint is the fixed upper limit of twenty-one million BTC and the predetermined schedule of coin emission that results in that upper limit. Let's consider the ramifications of bitcoin's steadily decreasing inflation rate (which will eventually be zero) and its fixed-upper-limit money supply.

A WORLD WITHOUT RISING PRICES

First, let's recall the inevitable consequence of an inflated money supply, which is higher prices. Conversely, then, in an economy using a money supply that does not inflate, prices will not rise due to inflation.[54] As we discussed in chapter 4, the natural

---

[54] There are other ways prices can rise, such as a natural disaster diminishing the supply of a good or increasing the demand for another good. But these are typically temporary and localized; monetary supply inflation impacts prices across an economy, and usually on a permanent basis.

tendency of prices is to decline, not rise, if the money supply is stable. Since everyone reading this book has lived in a world where rising prices are the norm, it might be difficult to grasp how decreasing prices impact various aspects of our lives.

Imagine you live in a world of noninflationary money and you're thinking about buying a new car. The price is currently $30,000, but based on what you've seen in this hypothetical economy, you feel confident that it will only cost $28,000 next year. Do you pull the trigger to purchase the car? If you really need the car, you will, but you'll consider seriously whether you *need* the car or just *want* the car.[55] The falling prices give you pause, ensuring that you distinguish between needs and wants. You are incentivized to save rather than spend. But if you believe the car will cost $32,000 next year, you are far more likely to buy it now, even if you don't absolutely need it at the moment.

The car example shows how falling prices (which can also be thought of as the rising value of money) slow down excessive consumption. A person will still purchase the necessities of life, and even many things he wants, but will be far less likely to waste money. Impulse purchasing declines,

---

[55] Some modern economists argue that deflation is bad for an economy because people will not buy anything other than the absolute necessities of life, thus stagnating an economy. Today's tech industry quickly disproves that hypothesis. Because of the rapid advances in technology, prices of items such as TVs, cell phones, and computers go down over time, offsetting the impact of inflation. Yet the tech industry is still one of the most robust segments of our modern economy. People don't refuse to buy nonessential items when the price is falling, but they do consider that falling price when making purchasing decisions.

and savings rise.[56] From a moral standpoint, this adjustment in priorities, spurred on by the monetary standard in place, is significant. Remember what the *Compendium of the Social Doctrine of the Church* noted about consumerism: "*The phenomenon of consumerism maintains a persistent orientation towards 'having' rather than 'being.'* This confuses the 'criteria for correctly distinguishing new and higher forms of satisfying human needs from artificial new needs which hinder the formation of a mature personality.' "[57]

A noninflationary money supply directs people away from an orientation toward "having" rather than "being," while an inflationary money supply such as fiat does the opposite.

Furthermore, bitcoin's fixed money supply and decreasing inflation rate impact our **time preference**. Time preference is the degree to which a person will delay gratification in order to receive a greater benefit down the road. Someone with a high time preference would rather receive a good right now than a greater good later. Children are notable for having a high time preference. In general, a four-year-old will always choose one marshmallow now over two marshmallows tomorrow.

Someone with a low time preference, on the other hand, is willing to forgo instant gratification in order to receive

---

[56] Saving is also beneficial to the overall economy. When savings increase, investment will also increase, as many people put some of their savings into investments. These investments then spur new innovations and products that will eventually be available to the public.

[57] Compendium, no. 360, quoting Pope John Paul II, *Centesimus Annus*, no. 36, emphasis in original.

something greater at a future time. A person who forgoes a vacation in order to invest the cost of one in her new business exhibits a low time preference.

Bitcoin specifically rewards a low time preference, while fiat money encourages a high time preference. Low time preference is the better attitude, because it discourages immediate gratification and encourages discipline and simplicity when it comes to material goods. Bitcoin can't force people to deny themselves instant gratification, but it does reward those who do so.

Because bitcoin has a fixed supply, purchasing power in terms of bitcoin doesn't decrease over time. In fact, if you look at the cost of an item in bitcoin over the past ten years, you see the price goes down, not up. Consider the following chart:[58]

YEAR	AVERAGE PRICE OF NEW CAR	AVERAGE PRICE OF NEW CAR IN BITCOIN
2014	$32,386	50.52 BTC
2019	$36,718	3.39 BTC
2024	$47,542	0.79 BTC

The rapidly decreasing price of a new car in bitcoin terms naturally makes a bitcoin holder hesitate before making an impulsive buying decision.

NO LONGER GAMBLING YOUR SAVINGS AWAY

Bitcoin also discourages the overly risky, gambling-type investing that has become the norm in a fiat system. This might at first seem a ludicrous thing to say, considering the stories

---

[58] BTC price calculated by dividing the average dollar price of a new car in the United States by the price of BTC on July 1 of the respective year.

of people investing in bitcoin to try to hit the jackpot. But a deeper look reveals that bitcoin rewards long-term thinking not only in spending decisions but also in savings and investment.

A common refrain among bitcoiners is "stay humble and stack sats." This means that the focus of those who own bitcoin is simply to save in bitcoin. In other words, don't let pride tempt you into greed; just save little by little.

How does bitcoin diminish or even potentially remove the tendency toward risky investing that's especially prevalent now among young people? Let's consider how people view investment today, in a fiat-based monetary system. High inflation—and its corresponding rise in prices—is so common in our economy that bank savings accounts are a joke. In many situations, so is basic investing in the stock market—choosing established companies which grow steadily but not rapidly. "Buy and hold" has become passé among younger investors, for fear it won't outpace rising prices. That's why many people, especially among the young, choose to increase their risk substantially in hopes of a bigger payout one day.

Trading non-bitcoin cryptocurrencies is one increasingly popular way to gamble on investments (we'll discuss the value of these other cryptocurrencies in chapter 9). Many cryptocurrencies increase (and decrease) in value swiftly over a short period of time—even more so than bitcoin. In an effort to make money quickly, people buy and sell these cryptocurrencies rapidly, hoping to hit it big. More often than not, however, the opposite happens and they lose money. Owning bitcoin discourages this, because it is far more stable, while steadily increasing over time in value.[59]

Unlike bitcoin, the price of other cryptocurrencies is usually based on marketing, or on the charisma and reputation of the coin's creators, or on hype surrounding its technical promise—not on the currency's properties as money. In other words, success in trading these cryptocurrencies is typically just luck and hunches. Thus the mantra, "stay humble and stack sats": don't get caught up in a frenzy of trading, arrogantly believing you can time the market and be smarter than everyone else. Instead, just quietly save your money, keeping more of it in bitcoin.

Another aspect of investment gambling is the use of financial *leverage*, which is borrowing money in order to invest it rather than investing with what one has saved.

For example, Alice has $1,000 in savings and decides to invest in a company's stock. If that stock goes up 10 percent, then she now has $1,100 in her investment portfolio. If the stock goes down by 10 percent, she now has $900. Even if the stock goes to zero, the worst she can do is lose her initial $1,000 investment.

Let's say Bob has $1,000 but he wants to buy $2,000 worth of that stock. He gets a loan for $1,000 at 5 percent interest and invests $2,000. If the stock goes up by 10 percent, his investment is now worth $2,200. After he pays back his loan (with interest), he has $1,150: $50 more than he would have had if he had not used leverage—a 15 percent gain.

[59] Calling bitcoin "stable" might seem like a stretch considering its volatile nature during its short lifetime, but in comparison to other cryptocurrencies it is quite stable. We'll address that volatile nature in more detail later.

But what if the stock goes down? Just as leverage amplified Bob's gains, it will amplify his losses. If the stock goes down 10 percent, his overall investment is now worth $1,800. When he pays back what he owes on the loan ($1,050), he now only has $750 left—a 25 percent loss. If the stock goes to zero, Bob loses his $1,000 investment, but he still owes another $1,000 plus $50 in interest to pay back the loan. Poor Bob—in more ways than one.

Financial leverage has the potential for exponential returns, but it can also bring about complete loss and bankruptcy. However, it's a temptation in today's inflationary environment: Why settle for only 5 percent in a 10 percent–inflation economy, when you can potentially make 20 or 50 percent or even more with financial leverage? If bitcoin is used as one's store of value instead, then following the simple advice to "stay humble and stack sats" can be enough to beat the inflation of fiat money over the long term. No leveraging, with its inherent risks, is needed.

COMBATING FINANCIAL NIHILISM

Bitcoin, therefore, can naturally combat the financial nihilism that leads to these risky behaviors and that we see rising among young people. You don't have to be an expert investor; you don't have to spend time researching a multitude of publicly traded companies; you don't have to get lucky on some crazy investment; you don't have to day-trade cryptocurrencies; you don't have to risk your house—all in an effort to keep your financial head above water. Just live more frugally, spend less than you make, and save the excess in bitcoin.

This is the same model used by countless generations under a gold standard, and it applies just as much or even better under a bitcoin standard. This is the moral way to live, as well. A father who has responsibility for his young family, for example, should not be pushed to risk his family's financial future just to keep up with inflation. He should not be forced to choose between two unattractive options: either take high risks with his savings or face a devaluation of that savings over time. The stress that comes with risky investments has a negative impact beyond the financial; there are too many stories of husbands who risked their financial future for a greater return and ended up losing it all. Just the stress of trying to stay solvent financially ruins many marriages. A world in which breadwinners can just save in a noninflationary form of money to prepare for the future is far more family-friendly than today's world of constantly devaluing fiat.

The fixed monetary supply of bitcoin also prevents the worst-case scenario of fiat money: hyperinflation. The Weimar Germany papiermark, the 1989 Argentinian austral, and the early-2000s Zimbabwean dollar are just three examples of fiat-money systems that failed due to hyperinflation. Governments were so desperate to escape a financial crisis that they began to print money like there was no tomorrow. Ironically, because of their actions, there was no tomorrow for their economies. Inflation rates began to reach absurd levels: 20 percent ... 50 percent ... 1,000 percent *a day*. Nothing destroys an economy more quickly than hyperinflation: imagine a loaf of bread costing five dollars one day, and then fifty dollars the next! Images of people taking wheelbarrows of cash to the marketplace come to mind. And as always, it was the poor who struggled the most, as they always lack hard assets such as real estate or precious metals to offset the rapidly diminishing value of their fiat money.

Bitcoin's money supply simply cannot be hyperinflated, since the inflation schedule is hard-coded into the software protocol. We can know with certainty the total bitcoin money supply today, tomorrow, and at any date in the future (or past). Since it is programmatically determined, it is reliable and scheduled. The immorality of a central authority hyperinflating a currency is prevented by design in bitcoin.

THE RICH NO LONGER FAVORED OVER THE POOR

A predetermined money supply increase also removes the possibility of the Cantillon effect, which favors those closest to the money creation over the rest of society. In other words, bitcoin doesn't favor the well-connected rich over the poor and middle-class, a feature consistent with the fundamental moral need to care for the poor.

Who is closest to money creation in bitcoin? One could say the miners, but they do not receive the advantages that those close to money creation receive in a fiat system. Remember, an essential component of the Cantillon effect is that new money injected into a fiat system by the whim of government officials takes time to work through the economy. The rise of prices lags the rise in the money supply, since it is impossible to predict exactly how much money will be created and when. But eventually it has its impact, disproportionally harming the poor and middle-class over the rich and well-connected.

The Cantillon effect is possible because new fiat money is added to the supply in a haphazard and nontransparent fashion; no one can plan for these additions and so those who receive the new money first can take advantage of their station. With bitcoin's predetermined schedule of new money creation, however, no such advantage exists. And mining is expensive, so those who receive newly created bitcoin often pay almost as much per bitcoin as any individual who just buys it on the open market. This differs from a fiat system, where connections, not work and energy, bring one close to money creation. In a bitcoin economy, new money creation does not favor the wealthy and well-connected to the detriment of the left-behind poor and marginalized.

Another advantage the rich have over the poor in a fiat system is their greater access to hard assets. A hard asset is something that keeps its value over time, even in the face of inflation. Examples include real estate and precious metals. Hard assets like real estate resist the negative effects of inflation since they rise in value in fiat terms along with other prices. If John owns ten rental properties, the value of his properties eventually rises due to inflation, so even if his wages stagnate behind rising consumer prices, John's overall wealth and savings keep up (or at least keep up better than if he did not have hard assets). The rich have always known this, which is why they always ensure they own hard assets.

But typically, hard assets like real estate are beyond the reach of the poor and much of the middle class because they require a large up-front financial deposit, which these classes don't usually have. So they're prevented from using this type of asset as a hedge against inflation. Yet, if the form of money is itself a hard asset—as is the case with bitcoin—then anyone, poor or rich, can keep up with prices by simply saving in that form of money. Again, bitcoin levels the playing field, which naturally helps the poor in comparison to today's fiat system.

RULES AND RULERS: WHO CONTROLS THE MONEY?

The list of the moral benefits of a fixed money supply such as bitcoin's goes on. Without the ability to create money out of thin air, governments are significantly restricted in their ability to wage unjust wars.

Right now, a government like America's has few obstacles to pursuing a bellicose foreign policy; if military force is needed, it can be paid for with new money creation. A natural check on war—such as the will of the people and their natural hesitancy to fight wars in which their sons and daughters will die—becomes impotent in the face of newly created money.

The United States spent $2.3 trillion during the twenty-one-year war in Afghanistan.[60] Yet less than halfway into that span of years, more than half the American public opposed the war.[61] This strong opposition had no power to stop the war, however, as the government could keep printing money to continue waging it.

A country with a bitcoin monetary system would be extremely hamstrung in its ability to fight unnecessary wars

---

[60] "Human and Budgetary Costs to Date of the U.S. War in Afghanistan, 2001–2022," Watson Institute for International and Public Affairs, August 2021, https://watson.brown.edu/costsofwar/figures/2021/human-and-budgetary-costs-date-us-war-afghanistan-2001-2022.

[61] "Most Americans Oppose Afghanistan War: Poll," *The Australian*, August 7, 2009, https://web.archive.org/web/20090810102232/http://www.theaustralian.news.com.au/story/0,25197,25895398-12335,00.html.

(note that truly just wars could still be fought, with the support of the people for special taxes to pay for the war). Considering that unjust war is perhaps the most immoral activity known to man, a monetary system like bitcoin that reduces its likelihood is far more moral than one (like fiat money) that increases its likelihood.

The upper limit and fixed schedule of bitcoin's monetary policy also points to an important moral aspect of all forms of money: namely, who determines the rules. While morality cannot entirely be reduced to rules, nonetheless rules are an integral part of any moral system. A moral code that has rules that punish stealing is superior to one that does not. Likewise, rules that are clear and fixed are, all other things being equal, more moral than those that are obscure and arbitrary, for clear and fixed rules give all people equal footing for understanding and following them. Canon 14 of the Code of Canon Law states that "laws ... do not oblige when there is a doubt about the law." This is a principle of all good law: confusing or secret laws do not have moral binding force.

Historically, forms of money abide by one of two types of rules: fixed rules of physics or arbitrary rules of man. Natural forms of money such as gold follow the rules of physics. Gold cannot be created in the laboratory (as the medieval alchemists found out); it naturally forms over time and must be painstakingly dug out of the ground. Laws of physics determine how much gold there is in the world and how difficult or easy it is to add to the money supply. Due to these constraints, typically the total supply of mined gold is only increased by about 2 percent each year. While more or less mining can change this number slightly, it's not possible for a government to flood the gold market simply because some official wants to; only finding a new deposit could do this, and then only temporarily. There's no way around the rules of physics.

Fiat money, on the other hand, follows the arbitrary rules of man. Since fiat is created by governments, the men who run governments can determine when and how often to create new money. They can even destroy parts of the money supply, if they wish to decrease the supply (they always seem to want to increase rather than decrease, however). With the advent of digital fiat money, even the slight restraints that came with needing to print paper and create coins no longer exist. The rules for creating new money, then, are completely in the hands of fallen men; there are no natural barriers. Further, in most fiat systems, including the United States's, it is typically a small cabal of unelected persons who make these decisions—almost always in secret and only later announcing them to the world. The process is both arbitrary and obscure.

The fiat-money creation process also violates the principle of **subsidiarity**. This principle, taught explicitly by the Catholic Church and accepted by many political theorists, recognizes that decisions should be made at the lowest appropriate level of authority. The president of the United States shouldn't be the one to determine Dubuque's traffic light patterns. The people closest to the issue are typically best suited to come up with the best solutions.

Yet the money supply of the fiat U.S. dollar is determined by the seven board members of the Federal Reserve Board of Governors along with five Federal Reserve Bank presidents. Twelve people set the supply of the world's reserve currency. There's simply no way they can know everything they need to know to make these types of decisions, even if they were always acting in everyone's best interests. If there were a hundred or a thousand men and women controlling the money supply, it would still violate the principle of subsidiarity. Simply put, any control of the money supply puts a group of people in a position beyond their authority and competence.

Bitcoin's monetary policy doesn't follow the rules of either physics or man. It follows the rules of *mathematics*. The creation of new money in bitcoin—and its upper limit—is determined by a software protocol that follows a mathematical formula. As explained in chapter 5, the bitcoin halving schedule results in fifty BTC created with each block for the first 210,000 blocks, then twenty-five BTC for the next 210,000 blocks, and so on. The actual mathematical formula and how it determines the total supply, for those who are interested, is this:[62]

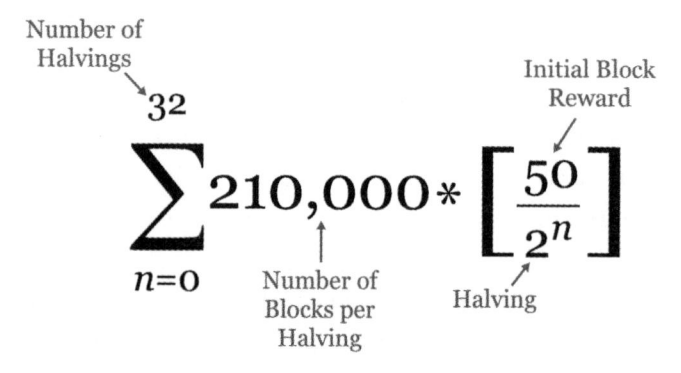

$$\sum_{n=0}^{32} 210{,}000 * \left[\frac{50}{2^n} \right]$$

Baked into the bitcoin protocol is a fixed equation which determines exactly when and how much new bitcoin is generated.

[62] For more details on the math behind bitcoin, see "The Math Behind Bitcoin Halving: How the Process Works," Rootstock, January 15, 2024, https://blog.rootstock.io/noticia/the-math-behind-bitcoin-halving/.

Unlike a fiat system, then, the creation of new bitcoin is not determined by individuals who may be swayed by greed or power or some other temptation common to all fallen men; the schedule is fixed by math. It's even more fixed than gold, since gold mining can be increased or decreased by men, perhaps without most people knowing about it. The total supply of bitcoin at any time is always known by everyone. The rules are clear and straightforward.

Bitcoin's mathematical rules, like rules of money based on the laws of physics, are part of the natural order that God created. God, after all, is the author of both physics and mathematics; both disciplines reflect our universe's ways of operating and the orderly nature of God Himself. While bitcoin, unlike gold but like fiat, was created by man, man used the natural order of mathematics to determine the schedule of that creation.

One could argue that since bitcoin is programmatic money, the fixed upper limit could eventually be changed; just a minor programming update could make this happen. This can't occur with a physics-based money like gold, where nature, not man, determines how much gold there is in the world and how available it is for mining. So it's not really mathematics, but man that controls the monetary supply of bitcoin, according to this argument.

Fortunately, the incentive structure built into bitcoin removes this possibility. Not only is there a fixed upper limit of twenty-one million BTC, the bitcoin protocol incentivizes all participants in the bitcoin economy to keep that upper limit permanently fixed. Consider who the decision-makers for bitcoin are: node operators, miners, and bitcoin users. In order to increase the money supply, the node operators in particular must agree to the change. But why would they do this? It doesn't benefit them; in fact, if they hold bitcoin (which likely every node operator does), then it actually harms them, because it devalues the money they hold. There's no Cantillon effect with bitcoin, and node operators and miners have no political power to wield. So the mathematical halving formula shown above rules the protocol, and everyone involved is incentivized to submit to this rule.

Bitcoin's monetary supply rules, set as they are by the laws of mathematics, are more moral than fiat's monetary supply rules, which are dependent on fallen man. They are even more moral, although marginally so, than those of gold, which can still be somewhat manipulated by increasing or decreasing the rate of physical mining. Due to the difficulty adjustment set in the bitcoin protocol, even ramped-up bitcoin mining won't change the rate at which new bitcoin are created. Bitcoin is independent of man due to its dependence on mathematics.

BITCOIN IS FREEDOM MONEY

At a 2022 bitcoin conference, North Korean human-rights advocate Yeonmi Park testified that bitcoin was being used to help people escape from her totalitarian home country. Most of those who flee North Korea are vulnerable women, who are frequently victims of sex trafficking. Christian missionaries in northeastern China work to free them, and often the only form of money they can receive to do their important work helping these women is bitcoin, due to controls in both

North Korea and China.[63] Bitcoin is literally freedom money for these women.

The independence of bitcoin is what gives it freedom to be used without third-party permission. There's no company to shut down, no founders to arrest. Bitcoin is fundamentally *censorship resistant*; it allows people to freely transfer money outside the control of oppressive governments.

Efforts by governments to control speech they find unacceptable have proliferated around the world. This censorship has impacted many groups of people, including Christians. Since the vast majority of governments are deeply secular today, religious groups, particularly ones outside the mainstream, are susceptible to the latest whims and fads of modern secular culture (which is more often than not anti-Christian). We see this in the rise of "woke" culture, which tries to impose on society views that just a few years ago would have been rejected by all.

There are many methods for imposing these beliefs, but "cancel culture" is the primary weapon: a person can be fired from his job or lose the ability to make money to support his family, simply because he states opposition to these new views. Another heavy gun in the arsenal of cancel culture is the ability to restrict a canceled person's access to his own money.

In 2013, the United States Department of Justice began Operation Choke Point. This government initiative pressured banks to break off their banking relationship with certain types of legal businesses, such as firearm dealers, payday lenders, and other companies that were considered at a high risk

---

[63] Alex Gladstein, "How to Dictator-Proof Your Money," *Journal of Democracy*, April 2024, https://www.journalofdemocracy.org/online-exclusive/how-to-dictator-proof-your-money/.

for fraud and money laundering.[64] At first this might sound reasonable. Yet many dangers are present if we look closely.

Some of the types of businesses that were investigated included coin dealers, fireworks companies, and home-based charities. It should not be hard to recognize how quickly operations like this can be turned into an opportunity for government officials to shut down businesses—and owners of businesses—they don't like. The businesses being investigated were operating legally; the government, however, used its control of the money supply (which allows it to control the banks) to "debank" those it opposed for ideological reasons and essentially shut them down.[65] This is not rule of law, but rule by tyranny.

An Orwellian effort like this is far more difficult under bitcoin. Since individuals and companies can hold their bitcoin in private wallets that only they control, they have no need for a government-controlled bank. And since the bitcoin payment network works outside the bank-based payment system, a person or company can make transactions with others without fear of being blocked by the government.

Some people might be wary of bitcoin's independence initially. Wouldn't it also facilitate truly illegal and immoral activities such as terrorism and drug dealing?[66] Perhaps, but

[64] See "Operation Choke Point," Wikipedia, last edited January 13, 2025, https://en.wikipedia.org/wiki/Operation_Choke_Point.

[65] Operation Choke Point was ended by the first Trump Administration in 2017, but the Biden Administration launched a similar initiative against cryptocurrency companies, dubbed "Operation Choke Point 2.0." The second Trump Administration ended that initiative.

[66] I'll address this objection more fully in chapter 8, "Objections to Bitcoin."

those activities are already occurring under the fiat system (cash has long been the most popular form of money used for illegal activities), and we have laws in place to fight those activities. Actions like Operation Choke Point are extralegal directives used when the laws don't allow the more aggressive forms of censorship some government officials desire. In an age when Christians are becoming increasingly persecuted for their faith, a form of money that slows persecution down should be welcome.[67]

HELPING THE UNBANKED

The decentralized nature of bitcoin not only helps the debanked, it also helps the unbanked. The unbanked are those who are unable to get bank accounts, not due to political persecution but due to having extremely limited financial resources. The poor around the world are not able to establish bank accounts and gain access to the financial services a bank account could give them. So they find themselves in a catch-22: ineligible to open bank accounts, but needing access to the services that a bank account could give them, to help lift themselves out of poverty. Involuntarily living completely off the banking grid hinders their chances to succeed financially.

Consider a woman living in poverty who has a talent for cutting hair and so wants to start a haircutting business.

---

[67] In 2023 it was revealed that the FBI had targeted traditional Catholics, simply for being traditional Catholics. See "New Report Details the Extent of the FBI's Weaponization of Law Enforcement Against Traditional Catholics," U.S. House of Representatives Committee on the Judiciary, December 4, 2023, https://judiciary.house.gov/media/press-releases/new-report-details-extent-fbis-weaponization-law-enforcement-against.

Without a bank account, she is unable to receive anything but cash payments, and she can't rent a salon. Even if she starts a cash-only business from her home, for example, problems with storing and securing that cash abound (never mind the licensing problems).

Yet anyone can participate in the bitcoin ecosystem, and anyone can easily store and secure his money. Since no entity controls the bitcoin network and all transactions are pseudonymous, no one is prevented from using it. This has particular relevance for unstable economies such as those of many less developed countries. In nations such as Afghanistan, Lebanon, and Pakistan, the number of people who use banking services is under 25 percent.[68] Even in the United States, the unbanked are around 4.5 percent of the population, including 31.4 percent of black households and 31.1 percent of Hispanic households.[69] Happily, more and more of the unbanked are using bitcoin as an alternative, needing only a smartphone in many cases to accept payments and even hold their money.[70] Using bitcoin for them is not about making a killing; it's about survival.

[68] Asli Demirgüç-Kunt et al., *The Global Findex Database 2021* (World Bank, 2022), https://www.worldbank.org/en/publication/globalfindex/Report.

[69] Federal Deposit Insurance Corporation (FDIC), *2021 National Survey of Unbanked and Underbanked Households*, (FDIC, 2022), 16–22, https://www.fdic.gov/sites/default/files/2024-03/2021report.pdf.

[70] Smartphones are becoming ubiquitous around the world, even among the unbanked. As of 2024, sixty percent of the global population owned smartphones. See Sunil Gill, "How Many People Own Smartphones in the World? (2024–2029)," Priori Data, January 1, 2025, https://prioridata.com/data/smartphone-stats/.

PREVENTING FRAUD

Bitcoin transactions are also far more difficult to defraud than fiat-based credit card transactions; in other words, it's harder to steal under bitcoin.

Current credit card payment systems use technologies that were created before the invention of the internet. They were never intended for use online. Although many people use their credit cards online without major problems, this apparent serenity is a false one propped up by billions of dollars of support from financial institutions—dollars that are ultimately charged to the consumer (that is, you and me).

It is now standard policy that a customer is not responsible when his credit card is used fraudulently. So, if someone purchases five hundred dollars worth of items from an online retailer with a stolen credit card, the legitimate owner of that credit card doesn't have to pay that five hundred dollars. Yet, the money was spent—so who pays for it? In most cases, the bank eats it as the cost of doing business. However, these fraudulent charges add up to billions of dollars (one study estimated \$33.83 billion in losses worldwide in 2023[71]), and banks don't truly absorb those costs.

Instead, they make up for them with credit card fees that retailers pay. If you spend a hundred dollars with your credit card at a store, typically the store only gets about ninety-seven to ninety-eight dollars, and the bank receives the difference. Again, this doesn't seem like a problem for the customer, as it is the retailer who must pay that difference. However, retailers

---

[71] "Card Fraud Losses Worldwide in 2023," *Nilson Report*, December 2024, https://nilsonreport.com/articles/card-fraud-losses-worldwide-in-2023/.

take these fees into consideration when they set their prices; they must mark up their prices to cover the credit card fees they have to pay. And who pays those prices? The consumer. So expenses related to fraud totaling billions of dollars every year are added to the cost of purchasing things, simply because our exceedingly outdated payment system is unable to prevent fraud.

One of the biggest flaws in our current credit card payment system is that the buyer gives away access to his entire account every time he buys something. You input your name, address, and all credit card details — number, expiration date, and the card security code — just to order a twenty-dollar book online. In other words, you expose everything a malicious person needs in order to use your credit card; and if it's a debit card, the criminal can access all the money in your account. Although this is the norm today, it's highly insecure, as evidenced by the many credit card breaches that occur in both online and brick-and-mortar stores every year.[72]

Bitcoin uses a completely different model for payment, one that is more like cash. When you transfer bitcoin to another person, all you give him is that specific bitcoin. He receives no data that enables him to access any more of your bitcoin. You don't even have to give him your name or contact information (although a seller may require you to do so in some cases). It's just like giving a twenty-dollar bill to the cashier — but electronically.

A bitcoin standard improves society in a multitude of ways, including combating inflation, encouraging discipline

[72] In 2023 there were 416,582 cases of credit card fraud in the United States alone. See John Boitnott, "Credit Card Fraud Statistics," Self, https://www.self.inc/info/credit-card-fraud-statistics/.

and simplicity, discouraging a gambling attitude toward investment, favoring the poor and middle-class over the rich, hamstringing rulers in their ability to wage unjust wars and enrich the well-connected, and preventing censorship and widespread fraud. Bitcoin is, simply speaking, a morally superior monetary system compared to fiat and even nature-based systems like gold and silver. It can't force people to be moral in their financial decisions, but it does prevent or at least disincentivize many types of immoral behavior. It is truly the most moral monetary system ever conceived.

Chapter 8

Objections to Bitcoin

If you told me you own all of the bitcoin in the world and you offered it to me for \$25, I wouldn't take it because what would I do with it? I'd have to sell it back to you one way or another.... It isn't going to do anything.

—Warren Buffet[73]

[73] "Buffett: I Wouldn't Pay \$25 for All the Bitcoin in the World," video clip from 2022 Annual Meeting of Berkshire Hathaway Shareholders, May 2, 2022, 5 min., 59 sec., Warren Buffett Archive, https://buffett.cnbc.com/video/2022/05/02/buffett-i-wouldnt-pay-25-for-all-the-bitcoin-in-the-world.html.

BITCOIN INVITES SKEPTICISM. Gold was a trusted form of money for thousands of years. Fiat money has been the dominant form of money as long as all of us have been alive. Bitcoin? It's not even out of its second decade; it's only sixteen years old as of this writing. What's more, bitcoin is a monetary system unlike any that preceded it: it's the first one whose money supply is based on mathematics. It's the first one that's fully digital. We've never seen anything like this, so skepticism is not only understandable, it's warranted. Is this magic internet money really all it claims to be?

Nearly everyone starts off as a bitcoin skeptic. When I first heard of bitcoin in early 2013, I dismissed it. Having been a software developer for years, I'd heard lots of claims that this new internet company or that new tech project would "change the world." The grandiose claims surrounding bitcoin seemed even more far-fetched—how could a virtually unknown, free software program controlled by no one become a global monetary system? It was too fantastic for my brain to accept.

Yet eventually I overcame my initial objections and realized that yes, this magic internet money really is all it claims to be.

Most criticisms of bitcoin arise from ignorance of the protocol or of how money works, although some do point to potential weaknesses in bitcoin. I've argued that bitcoin is the most moral monetary system in history but not that it's perfect. Bitcoin is still going strong after sixteen years, in spite of countless proclamations from pundits and experts that "bitcoin is dead!"[74] That's a call for bitcoin skeptics to take another look.

Let's help them out.

BITCOIN ISN'T REAL.

People have a hard time accepting as valid a form of money they can't hold in their hands. "If you can't hold it, you don't own it," say some critics, especially the proponents of precious metals. And in the case of precious metals, there is much wisdom in that saying. Gold you hold is more valuable than gold you entrust to a third party—such as a gold ETF (exchange traded fund) or a secure storage facility that stores your gold.

Even when talking about a government-issued money such as the U.S. dollar that is mostly used electronically, many people instinctively picture it as "real" money because they are thinking of paper bills and coins. In the back of their minds is the notion that in an emergency they could withdraw all their savings and investments and put all the cash under their mattresses. In reality, of course, most financial institutions won't let customers withdraw large amounts of cash, especially during any kind of financial crisis.

And there's nowhere near enough cash in circulation to cover the total money supply. In December 2023 the total M1

---

[74] There's actually a website called "Bitcoin Obituaries" that tracks all the times bitcoin has been declared "dead" in the press: https://99bitcoins.com/bitcoin-obituaries/. As of this writing, bitcoin had been declared dead 477 times.

money supply was $18.37 trillion, yet the total amount of U.S. dollars in circulation in cash form was $2.2 trillion, only about 12 percent of the total money supply.[75]

It's simply impossible to convert today's money into physical form. Most fiat money only exists digitally on computers, the same as bitcoin, except it took no work for digital fiat money to come into existence and it's not truly under individuals' control.

In many ways bitcoin is actually easier to truly "hold" than most forms of currency, especially government-issued currency. With bitcoin, if you have control of the private keys, then you have complete and total control of your bitcoin. There is absolutely no way another person can get it unless you give it up (either through bad security, under force, or voluntarily). Your money at the bank, however, isn't really yours—it is actually owned by the bank, and the bank agrees to give it back to you if you ask for it ... with a number of stipulations (such as a limit on withdrawals).

Catholics in particular can struggle with the digital nature of bitcoin. Our faith is incarnational: the body and the physical world are integral to our salvation. The Word became flesh, and the sacraments with their physical manifestations give us spiritual grace. What are we to make of a money with no physical dimensions?

Yet money is simply a tool we use to live in this physical world. It is how we purchase items we need to survive: housing, food, cars, prayer books. And bitcoin does "exist" in the real world: it is powered by thousands of physical computers

---

[75] "U.S. Currency in Circulation," U.S. Currency Education Program, https://www.uscurrency.gov/life-cycle/data/circulation.

around the world, and without those physical computers it would not survive.

The non-physicality of bitcoin is a problem mostly of psychology. As physical beings, we like to be able to touch and feel and see before we consider something "real." You can't do any of this with bitcoin. Yet it can be used as money to purchase items, so it truly is as real as any other money.

Many of our activities are now online—think of how often you communicate with your spouse or your kids through text messaging. Are those conversations not real because they occurred digitally? Letting the digital world dominate our lives poses real dangers, but in the case of bitcoin, this digital asset is supplementing our physical lives.

At any rate, religious people should actually be the first to acknowledge that things can exist and be real while not being physical.

BITCOIN DOESN'T HAVE ANY INTRINSIC VALUE.

Sometimes, when people talk about "intrinsic" value, they are thinking of some physical property an item has. For example, gold is said to have value because it can be used in electronics and is popular for use in jewelry. Or there's the idea that an item has inherent value that transcends our subjective view of it. Yet this is simply not true. What is the "intrinsic value" of your sofa? If you asked ten people what they thought was the value of the sofa (how much they would pay for it), you'd likely get ten different answers.

Anytime somebody wants something, it has value—and if two or more people want something, the value can be described more accurately as the most someone is willing to give up for that item. If Alice will trade two cows for a new tractor but Bob will trade three cows for that same tractor, we can say that the tractor has a "value" (or price) of three cows. If absolutely no one wants the tractor, then it has no value. No item has "intrinsic value" beyond what people are willing to exchange for it.[76]

Coming back to bitcoin, people have decided that it has value because it is an efficient way to store and transfer wealth. It fulfills the seven properties of money better than other forms of money. As long as people find it useful, it has value. Just like every money and commodity.

BITCOIN IS A BUBBLE, LIKE THE SEVENTEENTH-CENTURY DUTCH TULIP BULB CRAZE.

Every time the price of bitcoin rises, critics inevitably compare it to tulip bulbs. For those unaware of the backstory here, let me quote Wikipedia's description:

> Tulip mania was a period during the Dutch Golden Age when contract prices for some bulbs of the recently introduced and fashionable tulip reached extraordinarily high levels. The major acceleration started in 1634 and then dramatically collapsed in February 1637. It is generally considered to have been the first recorded speculative bubble or asset bubble in history.[77]

---

[76] Of course, I'm only talking about items that can morally be bought and sold. People, for example, have true "intrinsic value" in that they are made in the image and likeness of God.

[77] "Tulip Mania," *Wikipedia*, last edited January 19, 2025, https://en.wikipedia.org/wiki/Tulip_mania.

Tulip mania is the prototype of all subsequent financial bubbles, and so whenever any good rises quickly in value, whether it be Beanie Babies or tech stocks or bitcoin, comparisons to tulip mania will abound.

Is bitcoin just another financial bubble waiting to pop? Consider this historical price chart for bitcoin from late 2024.[78]

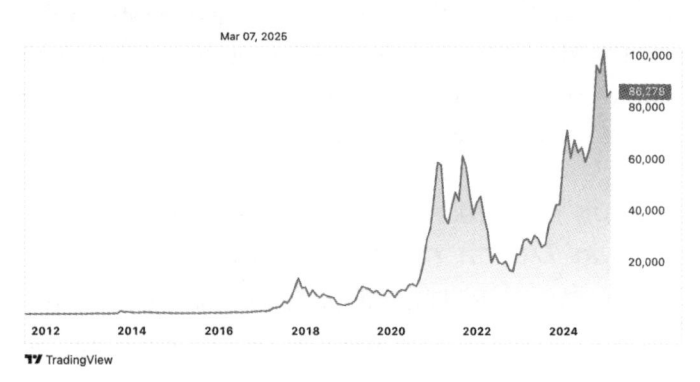

Bitcoin's price has enjoyed a dramatic yet erratic rise since its inception.

We see immediately that bitcoin's price is volatile (we'll address that concern below), but we can also see that although bitcoin's price dramatically decreases at times, the overall trend is upward. The following logarithmic chart is a clearer illustration of this trend.[79]

[78] Trading View, https://www.tradingview.com/symbols/BTCUSD/.
[79] A logarithmic chart is a graph that uses a logarithmic scale instead of a linear scale. Logarithmic scales create varying gaps between values, which is different from linear scales where values are evenly spaced.

Logarithmic charts are useful for displaying in a more compact way numerical data that span a wide range of values. Chart source: https://commons.wikimedia.org/wiki/File:Bitcoin_price_usd_logarithmic.svg.

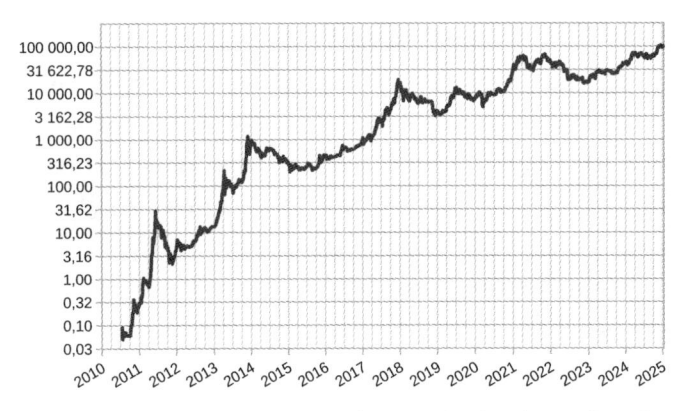

The logarithmic chart of bitcoin's price history makes clear the overall trend.

The upward direction of bitcoin's price is apparent here. This trend makes sense given all we've discussed about bitcoin so far. Two factors in particular contribute to the rise. First, due to its fixed monetary supply policy and its properties as money, bitcoin has come to be valued by an increasing number of people. The increase in demand spurs a price increase. Simultaneously, the money used to denominate bitcoin's price (the U.S. dollar) has been subject to ever-increasing inflation—which has supercharged the rise in bitcoin's U.S. dollar value.

When I first became interested in bitcoin in 2013, the "tulip bulb" objection had more power. At that point, bitcoin was less than five years old and still a fringe project. Its price rose from around two hundred dollars to over a thousand dollars in a very short time frame. Perhaps it was a bubble. But now bitcoin is sixteen years old and nation-states are holding it in national strategic reserves. At what point do critics recognize that bitcoin is no tulip craze?

BITCOIN COULD BE HACKED.

Software programs share a common weakness: they can be hacked. If we're talking about a game app on your phone, it's not a big deal. But if we're talking about software that runs a global monetary system and holds trillions of dollars of value, then it's a serious disaster if bitcoin is hacked.

So can bitcoin be hacked? I can't answer with a flat no. Because bitcoin is software, it's always theoretically *possible*. But bitcoin's design and history make it so unlikely as to be practically impossible.

One of the key features protecting bitcoin is the fact that it's **open-source software**. This means that anyone and everyone can view all the underlying code. Non-coders might assume this is a weakness, but the fact that it's a great strength has been borne out over decades.

More than 96 percent of the top million internet servers run the open-source operating system Linux.[80] This operating system is chosen by all the top internet providers in part because it is so resistant to hacking. Since the underlying code is open to the public, any potential flaws are quickly found and corrected before they can be exploited by bad actors. Perhaps counterintuitively, closed-source software such as Microsoft Windows is far more prone to vulnerabilities than open-source systems such as Linux. But if you've ever used both operating systems, you know this is obviously true.

For sixteen years countless people have been examining bitcoin's code, including some of the best programmers — and

[80] Steven Vaughan-Nichols, "Can the Internet Exist Without Linux?" ZDNet, October 15, 2015, https://www.zdnet.com/home-and-office/networking/can-the-internet-exist-without-linux/.

most malicious hackers—of our time. In 2011, just two years after bitcoin's release—and therefore when it was less reviewed and used than today and so more susceptible to exploits—one of the world's greatest security experts tried to hack bitcoin and was unsuccessful.

Dan Kaminsky had previously discovered a flaw in the internet domain naming system (a fundamental part of how the internet works), and he turned his attention to bitcoin. He failed to find a single weak point. Kaminsky later noted, "By all extant metrics in security system review, this system [bitcoin] should have failed instantaneously, at every possible layer. But the core technology *actually works*, and has continued to work, to a degree not everyone predicted."[81]

Hackers in fact are greatly incentivized to find holes in the code: if they own bitcoin, to patch those holes; if they don't own bitcoin, to steal some or to destroy the network. The incentives to hack bitcoin are likely more powerful than the incentive to hack almost any other computer system in the world.

Yet no one has found a hole; no one has ever hacked bitcoin. The longer bitcoin goes without being hacked, the more secure it can be considered. Bitcoin wasn't hacked in its first year, when the project was obscure and the value of a bitcoin measured in cents, not dollars, but that's no proof it isn't hackable. Then it wasn't hacked in its second year or third year or fourth year, as more hackers took notice of it and the value of bitcoin continued to rise. Now it's been sixteen years, countless people have analyzed the code, and a single bitcoin is

---

[81] Dan Kaminsky, "I Tried Hacking Bitcoin and I Failed," *Business Insider*, April 12, 2013, https://www.businessinsider.com/dan-kaminsky-highlights-flaws-bitcoin-2013-4.

worth about $100,000 as of this writing. Still it hasn't been hacked. Based on this history, the odds of a security hole being found in the code have become astonishingly small.

But there's another way bitcoin could be hacked: quantum computing. Quantum computing promises an exponential leap in computer power; mathematical problems that would take today's computers millions of years to crack could be solved, at least in theory, in minutes by quantum computers. More specifically, quantum computers could potentially break the encryption used in bitcoin, allowing a hacker with a quantum computer to siphon funds out of someone's bitcoin wallet with relative ease.

Remember public-key cryptography and the analogy of guessing an equation when all you know is that the answer is 7? Using traditional computers, guessing a private key when knowing only the public address would take so long the universe would end before it could occur. However, theoretically, quantum computers could one day achieve this in a matter of days, perhaps hours.

So will quantum computing spell the end of bitcoin?

First let's realize that if quantum computers can crack bitcoin's encryption, then they can also crack the encryption used throughout the internet, which, along with governments' nuclear codes, all use the same basic forms of encryption. The credit cards you have saved on Amazon would be open to the public, and the dollars you have deposited at Bank of America could be stolen, but all that might not even matter since the nuclear warheads at America's military bases could be launched. So quantum computing threatens our modern way of life.

But advances in technology benefit both attackers and defenders, and typically both sides advance in conjunction with each other. As quantum computing is developed, so are means to defend against it.

Left undefended, bitcoin could face a real danger from quantum computing, but quantum threats are not in our immediate future. Although sometimes we'll see media headlines screaming about breakthroughs in quantum technology, a closer look reveals we have a long way to go — likely more than a decade — before quantum computers could crack the internet's (including bitcoin's) encryption.[82] And we'll know beforehand if and when this threat becomes more imminent, which gives bitcoin and banks and others time to adapt their encryption software accordingly.

I have much more confidence in the bitcoin world adapting to this threat than in centralized banks beholden to inefficient government oversight. Banks and other institutions are typically slow moving and must answer to many conflicting interests. They have long approval processes and are filled with mid-level talent. On the other hand, every single person involved in bitcoin is incentivized to fix any potential weaknesses, and the project attracts some of the best minds in the field. Bitcoin is far better positioned than are large bureaucratic organizations to react to potential quantum computer threats quickly and nimbly.

[82] James Hunt, "Bernstein Says Quantum Threat to Bitcoin Seems 'Decades Away.'" *The Block*, December 10, 2024, The Block, https://www.theblock.co/post/330096/quantum-threat-to-bitcoin-still-seems-decades-away-bernstein.

SOMEONE CAN JUST COPY THE BITCOIN CODE AND CREATE A BETTER BITCOIN.

Bitcoin is open-source software, which means that anyone can copy and amend it to create a new version of bitcoin. In fact, it's already been done, countless times. The bitcoin code base is the foundation of thousands of other cryptocurrencies (which we'll address in chapter 9). Yet one of the key properties of good money is scarcity. Does the ability to create "another bitcoin" make bitcoin no scarcer than a fiat money? Or could another cryptocurrency just replace bitcoin and become a better form of money, making bitcoin worthless?

The **network effect** means the answer is no. "Network effect" is the economic principle that the value of a product or service increases as more people use it. Let's say I create a new cryptocurrency that I believe will be a superior form of money, and that it ranks highly in all the properties of money. That still does not by itself make it a form of money. My new "Sammonscoin" also has to be *accepted* as money by some significant subset of the population. People have to give it value. They must be willing to use it as a means of exchange for their transactions. The more acceptability a money has, the stronger it is, at least in terms of usefulness (if not necessarily morality—see fiat-money systems like the dollar). Some economists, in fact, consider acceptability another property of money, although I would argue that acceptability is the process by which a good becomes a form of money.

Bitcoin was the first cryptocurrency created, and it has continued to be the most popular cryptocurrency by far. The market capitalization of bitcoin—the total value of all bitcoin issued—has never dipped below 32 percent of the total market cap of all cryptocurrencies combined, and typically sits over 50 percent. Since 2011 hundreds of other crypto-coins promised to be a "better bitcoin," yet none have even come close to supplanting it. This dominance is called net-work effect — the size of its network gives bitcoin an inherent advantage over other cryptocurrencies.

My Sammonscoin may be technically superior to bitcoin, but overcoming bitcoin's powerful network effect would require massive resources — so massive as to make my hope of conquer-ing bitcoin a fool's errand. If I'd created Sammonscoin during bitcoin's infancy, maybe I would have had a shot. Sixteen years may not seem like a long time, but, as we're all aware, the tech-nology world runs on a different clock. Bitcoin is now part of the world economy, with millions of people, multinational corporations, and even nation-states supporting it.

Even though Sammonscoin is a fairy tale, many crypto-currencies that are technically superior to bitcoin in one way or another actually do exist. Some process faster transactions, while others provide more anonymity. But none have come close to bitcoin in terms of the properties and use of money. Those other coins' improvements came with trade-offs that undermined their status as money, most often making them less scarce or less independent. For example, faster transac-tions might mean the money is more efficient than bitcoin, but those faster transactions require more centralization, mak-ing the new coin less independent than bitcoin.

Bitcoin was a unique creation, a step forward for money. Making improvements around the edges of the protocol isn't the same as creating a brand-new form of money. Creating new cryptocoins does not impact the scarcity of bitcoin, as each cryptocurrency has its own money supply—we would not say the Icelandic króna is inflated when the U.S. Federal Reserve pumps more U.S. dollars into our economy.

BITCOIN ISN'T BACKED BY ANYTHING.

The objection that bitcoin isn't backed by anything reveals false assumptions about the nature of money. For most of human history, money was never "backed" by anything: gold was gold, silver was silver, and shells were shells. Only with the advent of, first, the gold-paper system, and then (especially) paper fiat money was there a need to say that money needs to be backed by something else.

Consider a transaction with gold. When I hand over an ounce of gold for a new suit, is that ounce backed by anything? No, its value is simply the gold itself. When societies moved to paper notes that represented gold, then people would say that the paper was "backed" by gold, because the paper itself was not valued as money.

In a fiat-money system, the money is backed by the government. Essentially, people trust that the government is strong enough and stable enough to back that form of money as legitimate and valuable.

Let me say that again. People trust the government.

In the short term, this trust in the strength and stability of one's government might be justified. But history has shown that often governments are *not* actually strong and stable enough to back a form of money forever. Let alone trustworthy.

The U.S. dollar is widely accepted today simply because people know that the military and economic power of the United States supports that dollar. This gives the dollar the illusion of stability. Why an illusion? Because all governments, no matter how powerful, slowly undermine their fiat money by inflating the money supply, and eventually all fiat forms of money will fail.

Money does not have to be backed by anything, unless the money itself is inferior, which typically only happens when a form of money is forced onto a people by the state.

So it's true that bitcoin is not backed by anything, just like gold, silver, and other natural forms of money. It doesn't need to be, because it's not fiat money. The absence of "backing" has no impact on whether bitcoin is useful or moral; that is, on whether it's good money.

BITCOIN IS TOO DIFFICULT TO USE AS A MEDIUM OF EXCHANGE.

Recall that money has three primary uses: store of value, medium of exchange, and unit of account. Currently, using bitcoin as a medium of exchange is limited at best and often difficult to implement. Very few merchants accept bitcoin, and the limitations of the network are such that bitcoin cannot come close to processing a high volume of transactions quickly, as credit card networks do today.[83]

---

[83] In 2017 there was a civil war of sorts in the bitcoin community as members debated whether to increase the maximum size of a bitcoin block so it could accept more transactions. Those arguing for bigger blocks said it would make bitcoin a better payment system and therefore a better medium of exchange; those opposed said it would harm the decentralization of bitcoin, as bigger blocks would mean fewer people would be able to run bitcoin nodes. After much acrimonious debate, the smaller-block camp won out, as node operators rejected bigger-block proposals (this, by the way, is a perfect example of the decentralized nature of

While this criticism is valid, it does not negate the claim that bitcoin is the best and most moral money ever created. If we think of bitcoin's lifespan, it's currently still in its early years; it's just a toddler compared to other, more established, forms of money. It's just getting started.

Historically, most forms of money have gone through "life stages," if you will, between the first recognition of a good as a store of value and its later use as a medium of exchange and unit of account. Right now bitcoin is in the phase where it is establishing itself as a store of value. Think of this phase as bitcoin learning to walk, with lots of ups and downs, but increasingly more ups. Just like a toddler, it's not yet able to function as a full adult; bitcoin is not used widely as a medium of exchange, and it's not yet a unit of account—you don't see many items priced in bitcoin.

However, over time, as more people adopt bitcoin, it will naturally become more accepted as a medium of exchange, which will incentivize companies, other organizations, and individuals to find ways that make transacting in bitcoin easier. We can't know whether those changes will happen on the bitcoin blockchain itself or on some adjacent technology, but as more and more people hold bitcoin, the number of people who want to spend bitcoin will also increase.

----

bitcoin control, since many powerful forces within the bitcoin community wanted bigger blocks, but the humble node operators did not). As of today, bitcoin can only process a small fraction of what the Visa or Mastercard networks can process, although developers are creating "layer 2 solutions" which would allow for a high volume of transactions outside the bitcoin blockchain that are later reconciled to it in batches.

BITCOIN IS TOO VOLATILE TO BE A UNIT OF ACCOUNT.

In its sixteen-year history, bitcoin's price has been consistently inconsistent. It has experienced price rises of over 100 percent in short periods of time, as well as price declines up to 80 percent. Even day-to-day, the price of bitcoin fluctuates. How can such a volatile good be used as a unit of account? Imagine a grocery store trying to price items in terms of BTC: it would have to update prices throughout the day.

Like the objection about bitcoin's current weakness as a payment system and thus as a medium of exchange, this objection has merit. It would be ridiculous to price things in bitcoin today; prices would fluctuate rapidly, causing confusion and frustration for both merchants and customers. But again, these difficulties are temporary and part of bitcoin's natural monetary life cycle.

In the natural evolution of a form of money, which of its three uses comes first? Were topaz stones used for exchanges first, or were they valued by the community first?

This is actually a vigorous debate with monetary economists and even within the bitcoin community, but the evidence suggests that, with the exception of a government-imposed money, a store of value is the first use a money must have before fulfilling the other two uses.

Think for a moment about a good organically becoming a form of money. Would people exchange something if it had no value? Would people price items in a good that no one wanted? If people believe that a good loses its value rapidly, will they want to use it to trade for other goods?

In the natural evolution of money, a good must be seen as a store of value first, before it will be used as a medium of exchange or a unit of account. (Government-imposed fiat breaks this natural evolution. This is because fiat is a *devolution* of money.) As more people acknowledge the good's value, they begin to use it for trade. Then, when a certain tipping point is reached and a large percentage of a population sees this good as a store of value and increasingly uses it as a medium of exchange, the price of the good stabilizes and other goods will begin to be priced in that good: it becomes a unit of account.

Why is bitcoin's value so volatile? And will this volatility ever decrease, let alone end? Remember your Econ 101: in a free market, price is determined by supply and demand. When demand for a good outstrips supply, the price rises; but when supply overshoots demand, the price goes down. Volatility in price comes when either demand or supply or both fluctuate in different directions.

Fiat money is considered very stable. We've seen that fiat money decreases in value over time, but this is a slow, steady decrease. The value of a dollar doesn't shoot up or down in a short time like bitcoin. That's because those who manage the fiat-money supply prefer short-term stability: they increase the money supply when there is more demand, flattening the dollar's volatility. But this comes at a cost: the long-term erosion of the dollar's value.

Bitcoin has no such mechanism; the supply increases on a fixed schedule. When demand increases, there's no corresponding increase in supply, so inevitably its price rises. But of course the price of bitcoin doesn't just go up — it can also drop dramatically in the short term. Why?

Price is an indicator of the value of something, and in the early years of bitcoin, people are still determining how they value it. This process is called **price discovery**: the determination of the price of a good through the interactions of buyers and sellers. Price discovery is naturally going to be more volatile in the early stages of a new good, as market participants learn more about it. And with no mechanism to change the supply schedule, nothing prevents this volatility for bitcoin. However, as bitcoin becomes adopted by a larger and larger segment of the population, volatility will decrease, since price discovery will be more mature. Price discovery is the natural means by which a good is turned into an accepted and truly stable store of value for a society.

As bitcoin becomes more commonly accepted as a store of value, it will be used more and more as a medium of exchange, something that has already begun as a growing number of merchants and individuals accept it for payment of goods. But we are still early in that process, so bitcoin's use as a unit of account—the final step in a money's evolution—has not yet arrived.

All evidence suggests that bitcoin's acceptance as a form of money will continue to grow, which means a steadily increasing number of people will use it as a medium of exchange. This will cause the price of bitcoin to stabilize. At what price and in what time frame, no one can predict, but when it happens, bitcoin will more commonly be used as a unit of account. At that point, people will no longer say, "Did you see the price of bit-coin?" meaning its price in dollars, but instead will say, "Did you see the price of gas went down to ninety-five sats?"

BITCOIN EMPOWERS DRUG DEALERS, TERRORISTS, AND OTHER CRIMINALS.

The first major use of bitcoin—when it was actually used as a medium of exchange and unit of account on a small but significant scale—happened on the Silk Road website, where people could buy and sell illegal goods, primarily drugs. This phenomenon resulted in two things: (1) it established that bitcoin could be used as a true form of money; and (2) it connected bitcoin to illegal activities in the eyes of the public. Ever since, one of the first objections you hear from bitcoin critics is that it's mainly used by criminals such as drug dealers and terrorists.

Bitcoin is used by criminals. There's no denying it. Does that make bitcoin inherently immoral? If so, then all other forms of money are also inherently immoral, and the fiat dollar, especially in cash form, is the most immoral money ever. No form of money has been used more by criminals than the U.S. dollar.

This standard is obviously ridiculous. Criminals live in the same society as everyone else, and so they use the same forms of money as everyone else. If a criminal is motivated by greed, then he will desire whatever good allows him to enrich himself and obtain the most other goods, whether it be gold or silver or fiat or bitcoin.

When we talk about what makes a money moral, we are not claiming that a form of money can *make* people moral, but that more moral money will diminish systemic forms of immorality related to the structure of that money.

But is bitcoin particularly better suited for criminal activity? Does bitcoin make it easier to engage in criminal activity? Yes and no. On the one hand, because bitcoin is easier for individuals to hold securely—it's better than trying to secure large amounts of gold or keeping money in a bank where it can be seized by law enforcement—it does give advantages to criminals. Of course, those same advantages are given to *all* citizens, including those unjustly persecuted by corrupted governments. No useful form of money discriminates as to who can use it—the innocent and the guilty, the rich and the poor; money does not care.

However, bitcoin isn't as useful for criminal activity as its reputation sometimes suggests. Remember that at the center of the bitcoin network is a *public ledger* of every transaction. Bitcoin transactions are not hidden; literally every one of them can be viewed by anyone at any given time. Many websites track every single bitcoin transaction. This arrangement is not exactly conducive to criminal activity.

Secondly, bitcoin transactions are not, contrary to common thought, anonymous. They are *pseudonymous*. This is an important distinction. An anonymous transaction means there's no way to connect the transaction with the parties involved; there's no public information that can connect any element of the transaction with anyone (think fiat cash). A pseudonymous transaction means that the parties don't use their real names in the transaction; they use a pseudonym, which can, at least in theory, be connected to the parties. In this case the pseudonym is the public bitcoin address of each party involved in the transaction. Users of the Silk Road site found this out the hard way. Many of them believed their drug purchases were anonymous, not pseudonymous, until police showed up at their doors.

Due to bitcoin's design, it's a poor vehicle for money laundering as well: the U.S. Treasury's *2024 National Money Laundering Risk Assessment* report found that "the use of virtual assets for money laundering remains far below that of fiat currency."[84]

---

[84] Department of the Treasury, *2024 National Money Laundering Risk Assessment* (February 2024), https://home.treasury.gov/system/files/136/2024-National-Money-Laundering-Risk-Assessment.pdf.

Let's say you're a terrorist and wish to purchase sarin gas for use in an attack. You find a seller and meet up with him. You each get out your phones; you send bitcoin to his wallet from yours, after which he gives you the gas. That transaction might seem safely anonymous, but it's not. There's a public record of it for all to see. Forensic cryptocurrency analysts can study where bitcoin flows on the network, from address to address, until it is used for something connected to an actual person. The seller of the gas, for example, might later exchange the bitcoin he received from you for dollars to buy a nice boat. By looking through the blockchain, those forensics guys can find the boat's seller and eventually track it back to you, the terrorist buyer. It would have been much safer for you to just use cash to buy the sarin gas, because it's far less traceable. That's why an estimated 30 to 40 percent of all criminal transactions today are done in cash.

Does bitcoin give certain advantages to criminals? Yes, but only the advantages it gives to anyone who uses it. It does not favor criminal activity over licit activity. If we were to reject forms of money that can be used by criminals, then we would have to reject all forms of money, and particularly fiat money.

BITCOIN WON'T WORK IF THE INTERNET GOES DOWN.

Bitcoin is 100 percent digital and resides completely on the internet. As such, if the worldwide internet goes down for any reason, bitcoin becomes useless. There's no denying this reality.

Imagine, however, a world where the entire internet actually does go down. Bitcoin is the least of our problems. Most of modern life is highly dependent on the internet; without it grocery stores are empty, gas stations are without gas, bank ATMs do not operate, and generally all of society shuts down. While it's true that people could not access their bitcoin in such a scenario, neither could they access almost any of their funds. All the basic necessities of life would no longer be available to most people. The harsh reality is that if the worldwide electrical grid goes down (which is what it would take for bitcoin to go down), then most of us will be dead, and no form of money will stop that.

Fortunately, the likelihood of a complete shutdown of the internet is almost zero, due to the decentralized nature of the internet. It was literally designed to survive in the case of a massive nuclear war (and bitcoin mimics this design). In the vast majority of future scenarios, bitcoin continues to run and is in fact a great way to retain value in times of monetary instability and crisis. And even if the internet goes down temporarily, the moment it comes back up bitcoin would continue to run right where it left off, without any loss of funds for any bitcoin holder.

BITCOIN WILL BE THE CURRENCY OF A TOTALITARIAN ONE-WORLD GOVERNMENT.

I've heard a surprising number of people make this objection. Since bitcoin is a borderless, global money, some worry that it would be the currency of choice for a potential one-world government. Hopefully, if you've read this far in this book, you already know why this is not possible.

The key characteristic of a one-world government is *control*. This, in fact, is why people fear its rising. In order to rule the entire world, a government would need to have extraordinary ways to control the populace. Thanks largely to technological advances, the means by which a government can control its citizens have multiplied dramatically in modern times, which is why an increasing number of people fear the development of a one-world government.

However, the money of that dystopian world, should it come to pass, will not be bitcoin, which is *decentralized*. With no owner or centralized system, bitcoin can't be weaponized. It can't be used (or manipulated to be used) to control people.

Bitcoin frees its users from undue subjugation to central authorities, whether the state or the banks the state controls. Since bitcoin transactions are executed peer-to-peer, meaning between two people without any third party, a one-world government would be circumvented, not empowered, by bitcoin. Bitcoin, in fact, is one of the strongest tools we have to prevent a one-world government from ever taking shape.

Don't be confused by the proposed central bank digital currency (CBDC). It would indeed be a necessary tool of a one-world government, but it's bitcoin's evil twin. We'll see why in chapter 9.

BITCOIN MINING IS BAD FOR THE ENVIRONMENT.

As we saw in chapter 5, bitcoin operates on a "proof of work" system: one must work—expend energy of some sort—in order to secure the network and be rewarded with newly created bitcoin. When bitcoin was first introduced, this work was relatively trivial—the average PC could mine bitcoin successfully. But as the value of bitcoin increased, the competition to be rewarded BTC escalated. Within a few years, the average PC had no chance to successfully mine bitcoin, as more and more powerful computers, specially designed just for mining, entered the competition. Now most miners are large organizations with server farms dedicated to bitcoin mining. These operations are expensive, and they use massive amounts of electrical power.

In terms of security, this is good news: the resources needed to mine bitcoin improve the security of the bitcoin network, because the mining process controls coin emission as well as verifies the legitimacy of all bitcoin transactions. If mining did not require significant resources, then bitcoin would be insecure.

Think for a moment about the security of a vault: it takes time and resources to crack into the vault; if the "vault" were just a cardboard box, security would be nonexistent. The resources required to attempt to hack the bitcoin network, in terms of both equipment and electrical costs, are becoming astronomical.

But the massive outlay of equipment and power does raise potential environmental concerns. Is the bitcoin network consuming an outsized proportion of power, to the detriment of our environment? If so, this would be a knock against its morality.

First we need to examine what we mean by "outsized proportion" of power. This is a fundamentally subjective standard: Who decides what's outsized? Virtually every service that man offers uses power—churches, sports teams, abortion clinics, and art museums all create carbon emissions. Who is to say which uses more power than it should? Militant atheists might object to the energy needs of churches, and Catholics believe that any power used by abortion clinics is too much. Likewise, proponents of bitcoin don't think the bitcoin network uses an outsized proportion of the world's power, whereas many of its critics do. It's a value judgment based on how much one values bitcoin. What is the worth of a global, borderless, permissionless, trustless, censorship-resistant monetary system?

Even before making that evaluation, we should look at how much of the world's energy bitcoin actually uses. According to one study, the bitcoin network consumes approximately 0.6–0.7 percent of the world's energy.[85] In comparison, air conditioning uses around 10 percent; refrigerators around 1–2 percent; YouTube consumes 1–2.5 percent; and televisions use around 4 percent of the world's energy. While substantial, bitcoin's energy usage is not a significant portion of the world's total usage.

Environmental concerns about bitcoin mostly gravitate toward its total carbon emissions. In 2022, bitcoin mining contributed around 0.2 percent of the world's carbon emissions, an even smaller share than that of its total energy usage. Most of the objections regarding bitcoin's carbon emissions are based on two factors: (1) a value judgement overall against bitcoin — meaning those who have made a prior decision against bitcoin looking for something to complain about, and (2) fears that the carbon emissions of bitcoin will exponentially increase in the future.

---

[85] "Crypto Energy Consumption and Crypto Energy Explained," https://justenergy.com/blog/crypto-energy-consumption-crypto-energy/.

This second factor is based mostly on misinformation regarding bitcoin. In 2018, a study alleged that bitcoin carbon emissions alone could one day raise global warming by 2 degrees Celsius.[86] This dramatic claim made media headlines and has been the basis for almost all further arguments against the rising emissions of bitcoin. It is one of the most cited bitcoin-related studies in academia.

The only problem is that the study has significant flaws and demonstrates a lack of basic understanding of how bitcoin works.[87] It has been debunked in a number of other studies, yet it continues to fuel attacks on the environmental impact of bitcoin. Some of these other studies even speculate that the total carbon emissions of bitcoin will decrease in the future, rather than exponentially increase.[88]

[86] Camilo Mora et al., "Bitcoin Emissions Alone Could Push Global Warming Above 2°C," Nature Climate Change 8 (2018): 931–933, https://doi.org/10.1038/s41558-018-0321-8.

[87] The most obvious flaw is that it confuses how transactions work in the bitcoin network and the role of transactions in the energy produced by the network. It creates an energy per transaction ratio and projects an exponential rise in future transactions. Yet energy is used in generating blocks (mining), not processing transactions directly. Since blocks are capped at around four thousand maximum transactions each and blocks are generated on a fixed schedule, any predictions about the future energy per transaction are based on fundamentally flawed premises.

[88] Examples include Eric Masanet et al., "Implausible Projections Overestimate Near-Term Bitcoin CO 2 Emissions," Nature Climate Change 9 (219): 653–654, 2019, https://doi.org/10.1038/s41558-019-0535-4; Lars Dittmar and Aaron Praktiknjo, "Could Bitcoin Emissions Push Global Warming Above 2 °C?" Nature Climate change 9 (2019): 656–657, https://doi.org/10.1038/s41558-019-0534-5; Johannes Sedlmeir et al., "The Energy Consumption of Blockchain Technology: Beyond Myth," Catchword 62 (2020): 599–608, https://doi.org/10.1007/

Furthermore, in recent years as technology has progressed, bitcoin mining has become far more sustainable. From 2021 to 2024, bitcoin's sustainable energy usage increased from 34.4 percent to 56.8 percent.[89] Criticisms of bitcoin's energy usage are outdated.

The bottom line is that bitcoin does consume energy and create carbon emissions, just like everything else that uses electricity. However, its environmental impact has been greatly exaggerated. These claims are a misleading way for critics who see no value in bitcoin to attack it.[90]

BITCOIN HAS CREATED WEALTH WITHOUT WORK.

Many early adopters of bitcoin obtained hundreds or thousands of bitcoin, either through mining when mining was cheap or by buying when prices were low. The bitcoin they obtained is now worth hundreds of millions, or even billions, of dollars. Though they invested little work or money, they now have generational wealth, wealth that most people only dream of. Some people argue that this is immoral — that wealth should be obtained only through work, not speculation.

Without getting into a debate about the morality of investment and speculation, it's important to recall — as I've now repeatedly explained — that bitcoin is a form of money, not an

s12599-020-00656-x; and Ashish Rajendra Sai and Harold Vranken, "Promoting Rigor in Blockchain Energy and Environmental Footprint Research: A Systematic Literature Review," Blockchain: Research and Applications 5, no. 1 (March 2024): 100169, https://doi.org/10.1016/j.bcra.2023.100169.

[89] "Bitcoin Mining: Usage of Sustainable Energy," Woo Charts, https://woocharts.com/esg-bitcoin-mining-sustainability/.

[90] For more data regarding the environmental impact of bitcoin, see the Digital Assets Research Institute at https://www.da-ri.org/.

investment. There is no company backing it, no stocks to buy, no quarterly earnings reports to study. If you own bitcoin, you don't own part of "Bitcoin, Inc.," any more than owning a dollar makes you part-owner of the Federal Reserve.

Bitcoin is primarily a store of value, and the point of any store of value historically isn't to confer wealth but instead to *retain* the wealth you worked for already. If that store of value happens to radically increase in value, it's likely due to outside factors (like runaway inflation) that harms your ability to retain your wealth outside of it.

Compare bitcoin to the most-used form of money in history, gold. Back in 2003 I had a little savings and so I purchased an ounce of gold. It cost me $330. As of this writing, that ounce is worth around $2,600. Although I didn't do any work to obtain the gain, I have an asset worth $2,270 more than it was worth before—an increase of 687 percent. Was it immoral on my part to own that gold ounce and hold it for more than twenty years—to increase the value of my savings through no direct work? Of course not. I'm simply doing what people have done for millennia: saving in a form of sound money. Neither is it immoral to hold another form of sound money, bitcoin, as a savings vehicle; in fact, I'd argue it is far more moral than many choices, for the many reasons we've discussed previously.

That being said, it's true that many people treat bitcoin primarily as an investment, trading it like a stock. There's no question some people buy bitcoin in order to strike it rich. They hope to obtain wealth without working. Their method is understandable, considering the wild price fluctuations at this point in bitcoin's life cycle (remember, we're still in the "toddler" phase).

Gold as money is thousands of years old; the U.S. fiat dollar is more than a hundred years old. Our toddler bitcoin, by contrast, is still a little awkward, sometimes falling in its attempts to walk steadily. This is essentially the free market working out how to properly value it: Is it worth $100, or $1,000, or $100,000, or $1,000,000? It will take years, maybe decades, for this to settle, and until then bitcoin will likely continue to experience extreme price volatility.

As with any good that experiences volatility, an opportunity exists to make (or lose) significant money. The very process of speculation actually is what leads to an eventual stable valuation, as millions of people determine how to properly value this good. Until then, however, it is not immoral to use bitcoin as a solid store of value and to save hard-earned money in this form. This is the virtue of prudence, not the vice of greed.

BITCOIN IS A CULT.

If you interact with proponents of bitcoin online for any length of time, you start to notice relatively quickly how passionate they can be. Some bitcoiners' passion is so outsized that they come across as members of a cult, trying to recruit people into their way of life. They promise utopia if bitcoin becomes the world's monetary standard. A common refrain is "bitcoin fixes that," where the "that" applies to *everything*. We should hesitate to embrace such over-the-top enthusiasm. Only God can fix everything, and He will do so in His own time. No monetary system will fix everything.

Though this cult-like embrace of bitcoin shouldn't be encouraged, it's understandable. We live in a world where

God has been increasingly pushed to the shadows. We are fundamentally religious beings, but we've ostracized organized religion. People have begun to look outside of established religions and to make up ones of their own—we see this with everything from fanatical *Star Wars* fans to the "Swifties" who adore Taylor Swift. Man has a hole inside himself that can only be filled by religion, but even if he rejects the world's established religions, he'll invent a new one.

What's more, without God, man's focus has been directed exclusively on this world rather than the next. Too many people accept these two assumptions: (1) God doesn't exist or is at least unimportant; and (2) man needs to spend all his energy fixing this world, because there is nothing beyond it.

In this environment, a revolutionary economic and technological marvel like bitcoin is sure to arouse passion among its followers. Bitcoin *can* improve the world, as I've shown in this book, and when you live in an era of financial nihilism, something as promising as bitcoin can appear as a life raft for people caught drowning in the sea of rising prices, bankruptcy, and corrupt government officials and bankers. Bitcoin might not fix everything, but it sure can fix a lot, so it does engender a near-religious following among some devotees.

Ultimately, we cannot judge something like bitcoin on the overenthusiasm of some of its followers. The *Lord of the Rings* books have many passionate followers—some a bit too passionate, as they treat it almost as a religious text. But their overexcitement should not diminish our legitimate appreciation of this great work of literature. Likewise, we must examine bitcoin rationally and determine whether it's a moral monetary system, regardless of the overindulgence of some of its followers, and if so, whether it is superior to our current monetary system. I argue here that bitcoin is superior in every way to modern money, and so we should support it, even if other supporters go overboard in their enthusiasm.

INVESTING IN BITCOIN PLAYS OUT THE GREATER FOOL THEORY.

Bitcoin is a form of money, not an investment. But let's play along.

Sometimes people talk folks into "investing" in worthless things. The Greater Fool Theory says the way to make money like this is just to find someone to buy the worthless good from you at a higher price than you paid. In other words, find a "greater fool" than yourself.

Okay, but *every* investment relies on selling it at a higher price. Why would I buy stock in Tesla if I didn't think that one day someone else would buy it at a higher price? Why would I invest in real estate if I didn't think the price of real estate would eventually go up, meaning a later investor will pay me more than I paid for a property? It seems like all investing operates on the Greater Fool Theory, doesn't it?

This objection only indicates that the person making it does not believe bitcoin has any value. However, any good has value if people place value on it, and the market has indicated that bitcoin does have significant value.

Imagine that a famous celebrity dies. At his house is found a chewed-up piece of gum. His followers realize that he must have chewed this gum and then put it aside. At an auction of his estate, the chewed-up gum sells for over $100,000. Does that gum have any real value? Not in the sense of it having any usefulness, but it does have value to those who bid on it.

Bitcoin of course has far more utility than a used piece of gum. It allows permissionless, secure financial transactions over the internet without requiring trust in a potentially untrustworthy third party, and it's a form of money that ranks highly in all the properties of money. So it does have value, which means that it has a price. That price might go up or down, and those who buy bitcoin may profit if it goes up or lose if it goes down.

The ethos of the bitcoin community also invalidates the Greater Fool Theory. Within that community is a strong mindset *not* to sell. When you believe that bitcoin is the best form of money, selling good money in exchange for bad money (fiat money) makes no sense. This follows the historically proven economic principle known as "Gresham's Law," which states that in any economy bad money is spent before good money. That's why most bitcoiners don't buy for the purpose of selling to a later investor. They buy for the long term, believing bitcoin will protect their hard-earned money from future debasement.

BITCOIN IS ONLY FOR LIBERTARIANS AND ANARCHISTS.

In the early days of bitcoin the community was dominated by libertarians and anarchists. It seems pretty clear that Satoshi himself was libertarian, based on his expressed views on government and the fiat monetary system.[91] Does this mean a person has to embrace libertarianism or anarchism to support bitcoin? Does bitcoin advance only a libertarian/anarchist standard of morality?

---

[91] One can read most of Satoshi's public writings in *The Book of Satoshi: The Collected Writings of Bitcoin Creator Satoshi Nakamoto* by Phil Champagne (E53 Publishing, 2014).

In this book I've shown that bitcoin is morally superior to all other forms of money, especially fiat money. I made no appeal to embrace libertarianism or anarchy in doing so. Good forms of money must make no distinctions among people; any form of money that would exclude certain segments of a population due to their beliefs would fail as money.

Clearly the embrace of bitcoin in recent years has far exceeded the small libertarian and anarchist communities. In 2021, the government of El Salvador made bitcoin legal tender in the country, and not only that, it began buying bitcoin as a treasury asset. In fact, as of this writing, El Salvador still buys one bitcoin every day to hold in its treasury. Many other countries, including the United States, are also considering creating a strategic bitcoin reserve, much like the gold reserves many countries possess.

While it's true that bitcoin received its initial boost from libertarians and anarchists, a far wider community now embraces its superior qualities.

THERE ISN'T ENOUGH BITCOIN FOR A GLOBAL ECONOMY.

Bitcoin began as a small project, with only a few hundred participants in its first year. Even after five years, only a few million people (at most) owned bitcoin. But what happens if bitcoin becomes the global reserve money? With more than eight billion people in the world, but only twenty-one million total bitcoin, it's impossible for even a small fraction of them to hold a single bitcoin. If eight billion people each held the same amount of bitcoin, that would only work out to 0.002625 BTC per person. There doesn't seem to be enough bitcoin to go around. Won't that put pressure on the bitcoin community to increase the total supply beyond twenty-one million, which undermines the most important property of bitcoin, its scarcity?

This objection reveals a misunderstanding of the difference between a consumer good and a good that is used as money. In the case of a consumer good, such as food or computers or houses, an increase in the supply confers a social benefit—more people are able to buy food or computers or houses, and to buy them more cheaply. It means a higher standard of living for the public. But an increase in the money supply confers no such benefit.

Consumer goods are, well, consumed, meaning they are used by the public. Money, on the other hand, is held simply to exchange for some consumer good in the future. By itself it confers no benefit on the owner, other than its ability to save value over time and be exchanged later for a consumer good. Thus an increase in the money supply does not benefit the public as the increase of a consumer good would.

On the contrary, an increase in the money supply leads to a rise in prices, which is detrimental to most consumers. Another way to look at this is to say that an increase in the money supply decreases the "price" of that money. If, before the supply increase, the price of a television was $500, that means a dollar is worth 1/500 of a TV. But if inflation leads to televisions costing $600, now the "price" of a dollar is 1/600 of a TV—the purchasing power of the dollar has fallen. There's no social benefit to this money supply increase.[92]

---

[92] An excellent explanation of why the total supply of money doesn't matter is found in *What Has Government Done to Our Money?* by Murray N. Rothbard, recently republished by the Mises Institute (2024). See especially pages 42–47.

But what about the problem of not enough money to go around? Can an economy really survive if the average amount of money owned is only 0.002625 of the unit of exchange? Yes, as long as the money is **divisible**. This is that important property of money that allows it to be used for purchasing anything from a stick of gum to a mansion.

In the bitcoin code, the actual unit used is what we call a satoshi, which is 0.00000001 BTC. This means a bitcoin is actually 100,000,000 satoshis. This also means that there will be 2.1 quadrillion satoshis in existence once the total supply of bitcoin is reached. With eight billion people, that comes out to 262,500 satoshis per person, on average. By comparison, the average global net worth in 2022 was $84,718, or 84,718 units per person in a dollar-denominated system.[93] (And no one worries that there aren't enough dollars to go around.)

So there are three times more units of money per person in a bitcoin economy than in today's dollar-based economy. Of course, money isn't evenly distributed among the world population, but that is a separate issue; the current situation shows that we don't need an enormous number of units of money per person in an economy. If bitcoin were the global money, there would be plenty of supply to use satoshis as a unit of account.

Finally, remember that since bitcoin is a programmable money, the supply can be further divided. Currently the smallest unit is the satoshi. But the satoshi could itself be divided into smaller units in the future. Even if bitcoin became

[93] Dorothy Neufeld, "Visualizing the Top Countries by Wealth per Person," Visual Capitalist, October 17, 2023, https://www.visualcapitalist.com/visualizing-top-countries-by-wealth-per-person/.

so valuable that a satoshi was worth a hundred dollars (which means one bitcoin would be worth $10 billion), bitcoin could be further divided for a smaller unit of account. Twenty-one million BTC is enough supply, and always will be enough supply, no matter how dominant bitcoin becomes. Because ... math!

BITCOIN IS NOT FAIRLY DISTRIBUTED.

Early on in bitcoin's history the world saw the rise of the "bitcoin millionaires." These were the men who obtained bitcoin in the first years of the project and, due to its rapid rise in price, held more than $1 million in bitcoin. Not too many years after that, many of these same men became "bitcoin billionaires" as the price of BTC continued to skyrocket.

This gave rise to the complaint that early adopters had an unfair advantage over the rest of the population. The overall distribution of bitcoin ownership was not fair — too much bitcoin was concentrated in too few hands.

Before addressing this objection directly, first we should admit one common motivation for this complaint: envy. It's always been true that some people are just envious that others are wealthy while they are not. The envious feel they deserve those riches as much as someone else, and so if they don't have them, they'll do their best to knock down those who do. We should recognize this as a vice.

That being said, some who voice this complaint are altruistic. They fear a huge gap between the rich and the poor, and so lament the apparent gap between early adopters of bitcoin and everyone else. Does their objection have merit?

Well, what's their solution? How *should* bitcoin have been distributed in its early stages?

Pretend it's 2009 and Satoshi generates the full supply of twenty-one million at the start of the project. What does he do to distribute those coins? He can keep them all to himself, but then bitcoin will be worthless to the wider world. He can give them to his close friends and family, but, again, bitcoin will be worthless to most people. He can give them away for free to the whole world, but if he does so, then the important proof-of-work mining system that helps give value to bitcoin and makes it "hard" money does not exist. Further, no one values a form of money that everyone receives for free. In all these scenarios bitcoin is a worthless digital token.

Or perhaps Satoshi generates the full supply and then puts them up for sale at one dollar per bitcoin. Who will buy it? Bitcoin is not yet a store of value, a medium of exchange, or a unit of account. And if it does start to gain value, then the wealthy will snatch up most of the supply, thus creating a truly unfair distribution.

No, the only way to have bitcoin succeed as a form of digital money would be to release it as Satoshi did: with anyone who wants bitcoin having to work to generate it, using a process that anyone could carry out. Satoshi himself had to use resources to mine bitcoin in the early days; he did not give himself an unfair advantage over anyone else.[94] Further, Satoshi

---

[94]   It is believed that Satoshi mined around one million BTC in the first year of bitcoin's existence, but those coins have never been spent (we know this from studying the blockchain). Whether or not Satoshi is still alive, and if so even has access to those coins, is an open question. What we do know for sure is that he has not spent them, even when the value of his holdings reached over $100 billion.

himself walked away from the project after two years, ensuring that he—and therefore bitcoin—could not favor any person or group in the future.

In the system Satoshi created, early adopters were rewarded, but they also took risk and initiative and did work for what they received. And Satoshi's system was also the only way to generate a sound form of money. The way in which new bitcoin is generated supports an equality of opportunity, but doesn't force an equality of outcome—that would be immoral. Anyone and everyone has the opportunity to obtain bitcoin, and that has been true from the beginning. Moreover, the distribution of bitcoin has steadily expanded; its coin ownership is far less concentrated than any other cryptocurrency.[95]

IT'S TOO LATE TO GET INTO BITCOIN.

I hesitated initially to include this objection, because it's not an objection against bitcoin itself, or against bitcoin as a form of money. But since I hear this comment perhaps more than any other when talking with people new to bitcoin, I realized it should be addressed.

Each time bitcoin's price climbs to a new all-time high, I hear the same lament: "It's too late for me to get in." The assumption is that the price of bitcoin can't go much higher. People said this when bitcoin's price was $1,000. Then they were saying this when it was $5,000, $10,000, $20,000, $60,000, and $100,000. Obviously, those who assumed that bitcoin's price would not rise higher were mistaken.

---

[95] Andrew Bailey, "Is Bitcoin Fairly Distributed?" Bitcoin Policy Institute, July 4, 2022, https://www.btcpolicy.org/articles/is-bitcoin-fairly-distributed.

I hope by now you can guess what I'm going to point out as the first error here. Bitcoin is not a stock, so thinking of it like one is going to steer people wrong. We've all seen limits to how much a stock's price can rise, but that's because a stock's price is constrained by two factors that don't apply to bitcoin. First, a stock is part-ownership in a company, and the stock price is typically related to the company's profits. There are upper limits to how much profit a company can make, even for the world's most successful companies.

The total value of all bitcoin in existence as of late 2024 is around $2 trillion. While this might sound like a lot initially, it represents only a small fraction of the total value of all global assets (which is around $500 trillion[96]). The total gold supply is worth around $18 trillion. As a potential form of money, bitcoin's worth is not constrained to a single company's worth or profits, so it can still grow dramatically in the future.

The daunting price of a single bitcoin leads to another, more psychological, reason people believe it's "too late" to buy bitcoin. Typically, when a company's stock rises dramatically, its board votes to split the stock. A stock split divides the stock into more units at a lower price. So, if the stock's price is $100 per share, when it splits each holder of one share of stock receives two shares worth $50 each. The overall value of the company did not change; instead, the number of shares increased. This is often done for practical and psychological reasons. Practically, if a single stock is too expensive (say,

[96] Boston Consulting Group (BCG), "Global Wealth Report 2024: The GenAI Era Unfolds," July 2024, 3, https://web-assets.bcg.com/0c/b4/1e8b9a66409a8deae6fc166aa26e/2024-global-wealth-report-july-2024-edit-02.pdf.

$10,000 per share), most people can't afford to buy even one share. Psychologically, companies are addressing the exact issue being discussed right now: they don't want people thinking it's "too late" to buy their stock. Most people don't follow stock splits, so all they see is that the vast majority of stocks are priced under $500 a share.

For example, a single share of Apple stock when the company went public in 1980 now equals 224 shares, due to stock splits. A single Apple share today is priced around $230. If Apple had never split its stock, the current price would instead be $51,520 per share. A price tag like that would scare off many investors, since buying fractional shares of a stock can be difficult.

Since bitcoin is a decentralized form of money and not a company, it does not have the same limits to its top price, nor the ability to split its "stock." Anyway, bitcoin's price doesn't need to "split." Yes, a single bitcoin has risen from being worth nothing in 2009 to over $100,000 by the end of 2024. Those who do not understand how bitcoin works believe this means they need at least $100,000 to "get into bitcoin." Yet, as we know, bitcoin is highly divisible, so a person can buy fractions of a single bitcoin: 0.01 BTC or 0.001 BTC or even lower. Some people, in fact, buy five dollars worth of BTC each day.

Some bitcoiners want to overcome this objection by using satoshis as the standard denomination instead of an entire bitcoin. At a price of $100,000 per BTC, one thousand satoshis are worth one dollar. Psychologically then, it might be more appealing to say that "I bought fifty thousand satoshis for fifty dollars" than to say that "I bought 0.0005 BTC for fifty dollars." Either way, however, the amount of bitcoin purchased was exactly the same.

SURVIVING THE CRITICS

Bitcoin has faced an onslaught of criticisms during its tumultuous history. "It's a bubble!" "It's for criminals and terrorists!" "Bitcoin is evil!"[97] Hundreds of "experts" over the years have echoed the *Star Trek* character Bones speaking to Captain Kirk, "It's dead, Jim." Yet bitcoin continues to operate exactly as Satoshi designed it. Its use and popularity continues to grow, and the critics continue to be proven wrong. Most importantly, more and more people are embracing bitcoin for what it is: a store of value and sound money.

---

[97] This last example is the actual title of an article published on December 28, 2013, in the *New York Times* by Nobel Prize-winning economist Paul Krugman: https://archive.nytimes.com/krugman. blogs.nytimes.com/2013/12/28/bitcoin-is-evil/. Of course, Krugman also famously wrote in 1998 that by 2005 the internet's impact would be no greater than that of the fax machine.

Chapter 9

Other Cryptocurrencies

> *Bitcoin is great as a form of digital money, but its scripting language is too weak for any kind of serious advanced applications to be built on top.*

—Vitalik Buterin, cofounder of Ethereum[98]

[98] Jacob Aron, "Bitcoin: How Its Core Technology Will Change the World," NewScientist, February 4, 2014, https://www.newscientist.com/article/mg22129553-700-bitcoin-how-its-core-technology-will-change-the-world/.

BITCOIN WAS THE first cryptocurrency, but it's not the only one. To date tens of thousands of cryptocurrency projects have been launched.[99] In this book I've argued that bitcoin is a form of sound money and the most moral money ever created, but what about all the other cryptocurrencies? Are Ethereum, XRP, Solana, and Dogecoin also forms of money? If so, are they and other cryptocurrencies as moral as bitcoin? Let's find out.

First we need to understand the origin of alternative cryptocurrencies, or "altcoins." When bitcoin was created by Satoshi Nakamoto, nothing like it had ever existed. There was no such thing as a cryptocurrency before bitcoin. Now new ones are created practically every day. How did that happen?

Because bitcoin is open-source software (architecture that confers the immense benefits we examined in chapter 5), it's possible to copy the entire bitcoin codebase and use it for another project. Anyone can copy and edit the code and create another "version" of bitcoin.

In April 2011, just over two years after the release of bitcoin, someone did this for the first time, creating "Namecoin," the first altcoin. Soon, other altcoins were created, including Litecoin, Peercoin, Dogecoin, and Ethereum (although Ethereum wasn't a copy of bitcoin as much as code

---

[99] In addition, millions of individual memecoins have been launched as of early 2025. We'll cover memecoins in a moment.

based on bitcoin). The motivations behind each coin's creation vary. Many were created to be competitors to bitcoin, but not all. Some have a completely different purpose. And some have no good purpose at all.

In the last chapter I noted that bitcoin is different from other cryptocurrencies due to its network effect. Being first and biggest makes a significant difference when it comes to being accepted as a form of money. I would also argue that bitcoin's history makes it unique among cryptocurrencies. Specifically, its founder didn't "pre-mine" — he didn't create coins for himself before they were released to the public — and he soon disappeared from the project. Other cryptocurrencies, however, typically have a founder or a group of founders that control the project, removing one of the primary moral monetary properties, independence, and often impacting another moral property, scarcity.

Unlike other cryptocurrencies, Bitcoin's history also demonstrates a marked disinclination among those responsible for updating it — the node operators, miners, and users — to change the protocol. This ossification would be bad if bitcoin were just a technology project, but it's a distinct advantage for a form of money (the fixed money supply is one perfect example).

We'll see that other cryptocurrencies fail in a number of tests of monetary properties, and some don't even attempt to be universal forms of money. It would be impossible to evaluate every single alternative cryptocurrency, but we can ask two questions generally that will allow us to determine whether a specific altcoin is a moral form of money like bitcoin. First, how are new coins created for the cryptocurrency? Second, what is the reason behind the creation of the cryptocurrency?

COMPETING TYPES OF COIN EMISSION

Cryptocurrencies generate new coins using one of three methods. Evaluating a cryptocurrency's coin emission methodology is vital in determining if a proposed form of money is moral. When a system's new money is created by a small group of people whenever they want and for the benefit of themselves and those connected to them, as with fiat money, that's a real moral problem.

The first method of emission is the one used by bitcoin, **proof of work**. In the bitcoin system computers must "work" by solving difficult mathematical challenges in order to secure the network and earn new coin rewards. The first altcoins simply copied this method, and many altcoins today continue to use a proof-of-work system. Although this gave those early altcoins the same security foundations as bitcoin, it did not automatically make them as secure as bitcoin. The size of the network mining the cryptocurrency is a primary factor in the coin's security, and bitcoin's mining network dwarfs all other altcoin mining networks combined. Here the network effect is paramount.

Another coin emission method is called **proof of stake**. Under a proof-of-stake mechanism, any coin holder can validate transactions and receive new coin rewards. Sophisticated computers are not needed for mining, for there is no mining; instead, simply owning the altcoin and "staking" it is sufficient to receive new coins. Staking typically means the coins are "locked" and can't be spent while in this mode. The more coins one stakes, the more new coins he earns.

The primary advantage of proof of stake is that it consumes far less resources than proof of work—no electricity-using mining equipment is required. Another advantage is that one can stake with far fewer up-front costs than mining requires. Instead of expensive mining equipment, just hold and stake your coins and you're part of the coin-emission process.

However, this process also means the altcoin is not "hard money," since no work is done or energy spent in order to bring about new coins. In a very real sense, it's just gifting new coins to existing owners of coins, which is a form of the Cantillon effect—those closest to the money production receive the most benefits of that production. Finally, it heavily favors early adopters, since they are better positioned to own a large stake of the total supply of coins in a project and so receive the most new coins.

Some altcoins don't use either proof of work or proof of stake. Instead, they employ a **centralized organization** to issue new coins and secure the network. For example, Ripple (XRP) pre-mined all its coins before launch. Then, on a periodic basis, Ripple Labs (the entity behind Ripple's creation) releases some of these coins into circulation, while continuing to own many itself. In essence this is a fiat-money system and so has all the advantages and disadvantages of a fiat money. Proposed Central Bank Digital Currencies (CBDCs) would likely use a centralized methodology like this.

When we look closely at the various methods of coin emission, proof of work is the only one that avoids the moral issues akin to those of fiat.

But there's more to altcoins. Looking at why different types of altcoin projects got underway will shed more light on them. Altcoin founders typically have one of six reasons they began their projects: as a form of money, as a stable-coin, as a technology project, as a memecoin, as a scam, or as a CBDC.

FORM OF MONEY

The first reason is the one most connected to the themes of this book. After bitcoin had been in existence for some time, developers recommended improvements to the bitcoin protocol — to speed up transactions, to improve security, or to improve how bitcoin was mined. The vast majority of these suggestions were rejected by the consensus mechanism of the bitcoin community, and the few accepted amounted to negligible changes. A few developers took their toys and went home. They created their own altcoins in an effort to build what they believed would be a better form of bitcoin, a "Bitcoin 2.0."

One of the most successful attempts to create another bitcoin was also one of the first: Litecoin, which was launched in October 2011. The founder of Litecoin, Charlie Lee, copied bitcoin almost exactly but made a few changes so that transactions could be processed more quickly and cheaply. Litecoin still exists today; some even call it the silver to bitcoin's gold. But it has not reached anywhere near bitcoin's network effect, and in late 2024 it had only 0.45 percent of bitcoin's market capitalization. There's nothing exceptional about Litecoin that leads one to believe it could ever replace bitcoin.

Another early competitor to bitcoin as money made significantly more improvements. Created in January 2014, this competitor underwent a number of name changes in its early years, from X11 to Darkcoin, finally settling on DASH.[100] DASH is actually a copy of a copy of bitcoin, because its founder, Evan Duffield, copied Litecoin's code, not bitcoin's. His goal was to pick up where Litecoin left off, making DASH a better payment system than either of its predecessors. DASH featured better built-in privacy, more transactions per second, and even the ability to make instant (less than one second) confirmed transactions. The ultimate goal of DASH was to create not only a new form of money but also a blockchain-based competitor to PayPal.

At one point in 2017 DASH was the third largest cryptocurrency among thousands by market capitalization. The price of one DASH rose to more than $1,500. By late 2024, however, DASH's market cap had plummeted—it typically ranks between 150 and 200 among all cryptocurrencies, and one DASH is worth less than fifty dollars.

DASH is a good case study on the ability of altcoins to become accepted forms of money, either replacing bitcoin or joining it in the marketplace of moneys. There's no question that DASH is technically superior to bitcoin in many aspects. It's much easier, faster, and cheaper to use for payments than bitcoin. Yet it's also clearly a failure. No one seriously considers it a form of money today. Why not?

The primary reason is what we've already discussed: network effect. Any cryptocurrency attempting to be a form of money needs to be accepted as a form of money by a large

---

[100] Full disclosure: I was significantly involved with DASH in its early years, including being a DASH masternode operator and a Trust Protector of the DASH DAO Irrevocable Trust. I am no longer involved and no longer own any DASH.

group of people. I might believe that Sammonscoin is the greatest form of money ever invented, but if I'm the only person who will use it, then it's not actually a form of money after all. Bitcoin, as the first, most well-known, and most widely used cryptocurrency, enjoys a tremendous network effect, greater than that of all other cryptocurrencies. The difficulty of another cryptocurrency toppling or even joining bitcoin as a form of money is staggering. People have clearly demonstrated a need for a form of decentralized, trustless digital money—but only one form, bitcoin, has actually been accepted as such by any sizable number of people.

Did bitcoin "win" just because it was first? No, the reasons the bitcoin network effect has grown and the so-called "improvements" of alternative cryptocurrencies have largely been rejected by the bitcoin community are more complicated.

Take, for example, DASH's instant-send feature, which allows a DASH transaction to be confirmed instantaneously versus the average 10-minute wait for bitcoin (and 2.5-minute wait for Litecoin). Clearly, this is an improvement. However, as with any change to code, there are trade-offs involved; in this case, the improvement in transaction time requires the addition of another level of nodes which have capabilities regular nodes do not have. These "masternodes" are controlled by a small number of people who own a large quantity of DASH (you need one thousand DASH to run a masternode). Thus, an improvement to transaction speed led to a decline in decentralization. A small number of users can control the overall network.

Bitcoin avoids the pitfalls of these trade-offs by remaining extremely resistant to protocol changes. If we were evaluating bitcoin simply as a tech project, this is a disadvantage—every tech project should be continually improving and adding features. But as a form of money, it's an advantage. The long-term consequences of significant changes are often unknown, and people want their money to be stable. What if an improvement in transaction speed means a small number of people can control which transactions are approved in the future? Or what if making such changes creates a small bug that is later exploited for the theft of funds? The proper attitude toward changing a form of money should be extreme conservatism, and bitcoin's decision-makers—node operators, miners, and users—are incentivized to be extremely conservative, far more conservative than other cryptocurrencies which constantly strive to "improve" in order to topple bitcoin.

So we see that while other cryptocurrencies can make *technical* improvements to bitcoin, those improvements are not improvements in the *monetary properties* of bitcoin; in fact, they likely degrade those properties. Bitcoin's supremacy isn't due to having the flashiest or most advanced tech; it enjoys supremacy because it possesses the strongest properties of money.

STABLECOINS

Stablecoins inhabit a strange place between cryptocurrencies and fiat money. On the one hand they are based on the same blockchain technologies that power bitcoin and other cryptocurrencies. On the other hand, they are not decentralized, and their value is directly connected, or pegged, to a fiat currency, usually the U.S. dollar.

The centralized entity—typically a private company—behind a stablecoin manipulates the coin's value so that it continually tracks closely, if not exactly, the value of the currency to which it's pegged. So, in the case of a dollar stablecoin, the value of one unit of that stablecoin will be one U.S. dollar.

To maintain the association between the stablecoin and an existing currency, the stablecoin's governing body holds cash and cash equivalents that match the total amount of the stablecoin supply.[101] So, if a stablecoin pegged to the dollar has a total money supply of one million, then one million dollars would be held in reserve. This allows the stablecoin to maintain its peg.

Stablecoins are in a sense a form of money, but more accurately they are just another digital means by which to buy, sell, and transfer the fiat money they represent. They possess many of the useful properties of bitcoin, such as ease of transferring value, but also the disadvantages of fiat money. If the value of one dollar is decreasing due to inflation, then the value of one unit of a stablecoin pegged to the dollar is decreasing in lockstep.

Essentially, stablecoins are a new payment layer on top of fiat money, improving upon the current bank and credit card–based payment layer already in use. As such they can be useful and a leap forward for processing current fiat transactions. But they are not a new category of money like bitcoin.

TECHNOLOGY PROJECTS

Many alternative cryptocurrency projects aren't actually trying to be Bitcoin 2.0. Their designers use the underlying blockchain technology of bitcoin to solve other real-world problems. They

---

[101] "Cash equivalents" means short-term investments that can be quickly converted into cash, thus closely mirroring the liquidity and value of cash. U.S. treasuries are the most common cash equivalent used for U.S. dollar–based stablecoins.

create tokens (coins) that are used within the technology project, often as a means to pay for its services.

The most well-known of these projects is Ethereum, released in July 2015. Originally created to be "the world's computer," Ethereum was based on the idea of "smart contracts." Smart contracts are ways to programmatically simulate real-world contracts.

For example, a smart contract could be responsible for paying out royalties. Let's say a musician releases a new album and receives three dollars for every download. Traditionally, for the musician to receive these royalties, the music company tracks the downloads, calculates the royalty amount, and then sends the royalties to the artist on a regular basis. A smart contract could automate this process. It could track the downloads and automatically send the royalties to the artist's cryptocurrency wallet. The artist does not have to trust the music company to properly (and honestly) track downloads, and the music company does not need to spend time and money tracking downloads and paying artists. It's all automated and guaranteed by the smart contract.

Ethereum is built to allow people to create their own smart contracts on the network, and it offers tools for making the creation of smart contracts easier and more efficient.

The biggest hurdle with a project like this is that the network could quickly get overwhelmed by spam contracts and programs. If anyone can upload and run a program on the network, then just about everyone will, and soon the network becomes overwhelmed and unusable. Enter Ether (ETH), a form of money designed for use within the Ethereum network. This token helps mitigate spam, because users pay Ether to use the network. This type of crypto is akin to the digital tokens many video games use for buying items within the video game world.

However, unlike video game tokens, Ether immediately gained real-world value, as people believed owning ETH was a way to be part of this intriguing new project. Ether began trading on cryptocurrency exchanges, and excitement for the project became so widespread that the price of ETH skyrocketed. It quickly became the second-largest cryptocurrency by market capitalization behind bitcoin. It's stayed solidly in that position to the present, far ahead of any other cryptocurrency trying to take its place.

So does this mean that Ether is a legitimate form of digital money, second only to bitcoin? Yes and no. Obviously it's being used as money within the Ethereum ecosystem, but it was never designed to be a universal form of money. Remember that a sound and truly moral form of money can't be controlled by any person or entity. Yet Ether is under the control of a single entity. Its coin emission schedule can be and has been changed by its developers, and many of those same developers received pre-mined coins before they were released to the public.

The project is centralized in other ways, too. The main founder of Ethereum, Vitalik Buterin, is still involved in the project and has huge sway over its direction (he also holds a large amount of ETH). Holders of ETH must trust that Buterin will guide the direction of the Ethereum project wisely and that the frequent updates to the code won't eventually introduce significant bugs.[102]

---

[102] In 2016 a bug in a third-party Ethereum project (The DAO) allowed the theft of a large quantity of Ethereum. Ethereum's leaders decided to erase this theft by altering the blockchain history so

Because of these factors, Ethereum's token ETH simply doesn't rank anywhere nearly as high as bitcoin in the various properties of money. This should come as no surprise, since the designers of ETH didn't originally intend to make it a universal form of money.

Since Ethereum was released, countless other altcoins have also been created as tokens for technology projects: some with the intention of being the "world's computer" in competition with Ethereum, and others for specific niche applications, such as decentralized, blockchain-based alternatives to Google and YouTube. In each case, the project tokens are eventually traded on cryptocurrency exchanges, so they have a real-world price attached to them. Some of these tokens keep their value for years, while most end up as worthless mementos of failed projects.

At one point "blockchain" was the latest buzzword in the wider business world; people would talk as if every technology project, and even non-technology projects, would eventually move to the blockchain. This was always a fantasy, however. In many ways a blockchain is highly inefficient and inferior to a centralized database. With a blockchain you have many copies of the same data, with lots of processing power and interactions happening to keep the blockchain up-to-date. A centralized database, on the other hand, has proven over time to be a simple and efficient way to store

that it appeared never to have happened. Those who opposed this decision forked the Ethereum code into another chain, Ethereum Classic, which maintained the original, unaltered history of the Ethereum blockchain. Critics of the blockchain alteration point to the altering of the original ETH blockchain as proof that ETH isn't a trustless, decentralized form of money.

data. When it comes to a secure form of money, blockchain technology offers advantages over a centralized database, which we've already detailed. But when it comes to just about anything else, it's not been shown that blockchain technology actually is an advance. The jury's still out.

In essence, these technology project–based altcoins should be considered more similar to stocks in technology companies than competitors to bitcoin as a form of money. Some of these projects might find real-world applications and succeed. Many more will fail. Like any tech stock, the price may dramatically rise or fall, and most will go to zero in time. Anyone can invest and speculate in these cryptocurrency projects, but their underlying tokens will never be widespread forms of money.

MEMECOINS

Memecoins are a type of cryptocurrency inspired by an internet meme,[103] character, or trend. The most famous memecoin is Dogecoin, which was inspired by the meme of a Shiba Inu dog thinking something in broken English. Yeah, really.

Memecoins are a way to represent an enthusiastic online community, and their value can escalate rapidly. Typically, these coins have no use case other than as a trading vehicle; they are not intended to be an alternative to bitcoin as a universal form of money, and they don't power any technology project. They just exist to trade and encourage enthusiasm for

---

[103] In case you don't know what a meme is, it is "an image, video, piece of text, etc., typically humorous in nature, that is copied and spread rapidly by internet users, often with slight variations" (Google's English dictionary, provided by Oxford Languages). But if you've been on the internet at all in the past decade, you likely knew that.

the connected meme. One could compare them to a digital form of Pokémon cards (a craze in the late 1990s).

Days before his second inauguration, Donald Trump released a "$TRUMP" memecoin. It quickly skyrocketed in value, reaching more than $12 billion in market capitalization. It was a perfect example of an exuberant community wanting to be associated with a movement.

As memecoins' popularity has soared, however, the coins have become more than just a vehicle for uniting a fanbase. Now people day-trade memecoins in hopes of hitting pay dirt. In this use case, memecoins are just vehicles for gambling.

Regardless of whether memecoins are used for building community or for gambling, they are obviously not forms of money.

SCAMS

While it's common to call any cryptocurrency project that fails a scam, many begin with honest intentions. Sadly, however, some altcoins are created solely to scam gullible supporters. The designers of scam altcoins "pump and dump" — intensely market and promote the coin when it is released in order to drive the price up, then sell it (dump) when the price is high and exit the project. Memecoins are commonly used for these scams, but some altcoins are marketed as the tokens for technology projects yet are actually just attempts to take money from the gullible.

Obviously these schemes are intrinsically immoral and constitute theft and fraud. It's hard to say what percentage of altcoins are true scams, but enough exist out there that anyone considering speculating in altcoins would do well to be cautious.

CENTRAL BANK DIGITAL CURRENCIES

If you think altcoin scams are bad, buckle up for the central bank digital currency (CBDC). It's easily the most immoral form of cryptocurrency (even more immoral than scams).[104]

Three CBDC projects have been launched as of late 2024, and hundreds of countries are considering implementing them in the future.[105] CBDCs threaten to be one of the most substantial attacks on human freedom in history: a CBDC takes all the evils of fiat money and supercharges them.

What's a CBDC? It's a digital form of money that uses much of the blockchain technology of bitcoin but gives one entity—a country's central bank—total control. CBDCs are promoted to the public as the next evolution of fiat money, particularly when it comes to payments.

I mentioned earlier that our credit card system is outdated, having originated in the 1950s before the internet even existed. So we currently have what was originally a paper and coin system, using a payment network that predates modern computers, all stuffed on top of the internet. CBDCs promise to be far more efficient than credit cards and paper cash and coins, allowing citizens to make payments and receive money much more efficiently than they can now.

That efficiency, however, comes at a serious moral cost (just as the transition to the more efficient fiat money from precious metals came with moral costs). All the problems of

---

[104] Technically, CBDCs are not cryptocurrencies, as they are commonly understood. They are not decentralized, and they are issued by a central bank. But for our purposes we can lump them together with other altcoins.

[105] See the Atlantic Council's Central Bank Digital Currency Tracker: https://www.atlanticcouncil.org/cbdctracker/.

fiat money, particularly as they relate to money creation and inflation, would still exist under CBDCs, since a central bank would retain its power to create new money out of thin air on a whim. But under CBDCs, central banks would also have the power of complete *control* over how money flows, down to the individual level.

To the promoters of CBDCs—who are typically the politically powerful—this control is a feature, not a bug. They tout it as a way to reduce criminal activities such as terrorism and drug dealing. Yet this control would go much further, of course.

Perhaps a person expresses opinions critical of the government on social media, or he promotes views unpopular with the general population. Under a CBDC system, the government could restrict how that person spends his money. Perhaps he'd be barred from spending it at a gun shop or for gas to travel to a protest. Countries like China already issue "social credit scores," which evaluate the "trustworthiness" of citizens and then reward (or punish) them accordingly. These punishments might include being socially outcast or losing a job, but what if the government could in addition control the money of those deemed "untrustworthy"? The implications are chilling.

CBDCs could also be used to implement economic policies. Perhaps a government wants to encourage more spending, incorrectly believing it will help the country's economy. It could implement a rule that everyone must spend at least 90 percent of his paycheck within sixty days of receiving it. This doesn't just become another law to be enforced by police; the government can change the CBDC system to make it happen.

Now money not spent in the time period allotted automatically disappears. There's nothing a citizen can do to stop it; the government has total control over money, which means total control over almost every aspect of life.

If bitcoin is the most moral form of money, then surely CBDCs are the most immoral—bitcoin's evil twin indeed.

To date, tens of thousands of alternative cryptocurrency projects have been created for a wide variety of reasons. But it's become clear that bitcoin is unique; it is *sui juris*. Of all the cryptocurrencies, only one—the original one—boasts all the properties needed to make it a sound, universal, and moral form of money.

Chapter 10

Getting Started with Bitcoin

Not your keys, not your coins.

—A common bitcoiner saying

IN THIS BOOK I have argued, I hope in a convincing fashion, that bitcoin is the most moral form of money ever used. Even assuming this is true, that doesn't mean bitcoin will be a *successful* form of money. It's possible, although no longer probable, that something will happen to undermine bitcoin. It might even flame out completely one day. Right now our world is dominated by a deeply immoral and imperfect form of money (fiat); just being a new and superior form of money doesn't give bitcoin any guarantees.

All of this is to say that this book should not be taken as investment advice (again: bitcoin is a form of money, not an investment!). Full disclosure: I do hold some bitcoin and so its price rise does directly benefit me. The views in this book are my personal opinion and should be treated as such. That being said, I know that many people are intrigued by bitcoin, and reading this book may put a reader in that camp, so in this chapter I give some practical pointers on how to safely and securely buy, sell, and hold bitcoin.

Keep in mind that while the bitcoin network itself is essentially impossible to hack and won't accidentally lose BTC or send it to the wrong person, the same is not true of *users* of bitcoin. Over the years many BTC holders have lost their bitcoin due to user error or some other human failing. Perhaps a scammer was able to convince a BTC holder to give up his seed phrase (never give up your seed phrase!). Or perhaps a bitcoin exchange—a company that facilitates the buying and selling of bitcoin—was hacked due to its poor security measures. In neither case was bitcoin itself hacked. By following proper procedures for using and holding bitcoin, users can avoid these pitfalls.

"Be your own bank," bitcoiners will tell you, highlighting the fact that unless you choose otherwise, no one has control over your bitcoin but you. It's empowering! But also frightening. If you're your own bank, that means a bank can't take your money, but it also means you must secure your funds just like a bank has to. If you hold your own bitcoin, you take on a high level of personal responsibility, since you're not outsourcing security to a third party like a bank. However, we will see that there are third-party options for holding bitcoin, which have their own advantages and disadvantages.

Another point to consider: the vast majority of the content and arguments of this book will apply as long as bitcoin exists. However, this particular chapter will likely become somewhat outdated within a few years. The companies that offer bitcoin services come and go, and so specific services mentioned here may eventually no longer be available. The ways in which bitcoin is secured may evolve. Further, I make no endorsement of any specific company; each one has a good reputation as of the time of this writing, but that's no guarantee of future success. When getting started with bitcoin, always do your own research in addition to what you read here.

Now that the disclaimers are over, let's get started with bitcoin.

BITCOIN EXCHANGES

So let's buy some bitcoin.[106] This means we need a **bitcoin exchange**.

A bitcoin exchange is a company providing a service that allows people to buy bitcoin; that is, to exchange dollars (or other currency) for bitcoin. A few exchanges offer only bitcoin for sale, but most exchanges also make available other forms of cryptocurrency, and on these exchanges one can also trade between cryptocurrencies. For our purposes, however, we'll focus on obtaining bitcoin.

To buy bitcoin, you need to set up an account at the exchange, and most exchanges also require you to identify yourself with personal information such as your date of birth and Social Security number. You may also need to upload an image of a government ID. This demand for personal information doesn't have anything to do with bitcoin per se. It's a result of "Know Your Customer" (KYC) laws that American jurisdictions have on the books. KYC laws require companies such as banks and other financial institutions (including bitcoin exchanges) to record customers' personal information, in an effort to prevent money laundering and other crimes. Once your account is set up and approved, you link your bank account, and then you can buy bitcoin.

Bitcoin exchanges have a checkered past, even though bitcoin's "past" is quite short. Many have gone bankrupt, with customers losing any cryptocurrency stored on the exchange;

---

[106] We are only going to consider buying actual bitcoin and not something like bitcoin ETFs, which allow someone to own a security that tracks the price of bitcoin but does not include direct ownership of bitcoin itself.

some have been hacked, with large amounts of bitcoin stolen; and some turned out to be elaborate schemes for stealing customers' money.[107] So it's important to evaluate an exchange before doing business with it, a little bit like thinking twice before giving your credit card info to just anybody. Some of the longest-running and most popular U.S. exchanges include Coinbase (coinbase.com), Gemini (gemini.com), and Kraken (kraken.com), each of which facilitates the buying, selling, and trading of bitcoin and many other cryptocurrencies.

Using an exchange that sells multiple cryptocurrencies has its disadvantages. Each cryptocurrency offered opens a new vector of attack against the exchange, which potentially reduces its security against hackers. Further, the deluge of cryptocurrencies offered can confuse many customers, putting bitcoin and a plethora of inferior coins, including memecoins and even some scam coins, on the same playing field. Logging into an exchange and noticing a new altcoin that's up 100 percent in the past day can tempt people to sell their bitcoin for what will likely be a flash in the pan. For these reasons, some exchanges offer only bitcoin to customers. Two well-known bitcoin-only exchanges are River (river.com) and Strike (strike.me). Although I've personally used many different exchanges in the past, I prefer the bitcoin-only exchanges for their simplicity and focus on bitcoin.

[107] In the early years of bitcoin, the most dominant exchange was Mt. Gox, where the vast majority of bitcoin was bought and sold. In February 2014 Mt. Gox went under, with the company's CEO claiming that most of the bitcoin held on the exchange had been stolen in a hack (he even falsely claimed the hack was due to an error in the bitcoin protocol, when it was really his own incompetence). Customers who held bitcoin at Mt. Gox lost all their funds.

Bitcoin can also be purchased outside of an exchange. Popular mainstream services such as Paypal and Cash App now allow purchasing bitcoin. You can even find bitcoin ATMs at gas stations and convenience stores, but I don't recommend these, as the cost of bitcoin is usually marked up substantially.

SELF-CUSTODY OR CUSTODIAL SERVICE?

No matter where you buy bitcoin, the most important decision to make is whether you will **self-custody** or use a **custodial service** to hold your bitcoin. Each choice has its own advantages and disadvantages.

To self-custody (in the bitcoin world, this term can be used as a verb) means being responsible for holding the bitcoin yourself; you can't lose your bitcoin due to the incompetence, negligence, or dishonesty of a custodial service. If you buy bitcoin at an exchange and immediately move it off to self-custody, then if that exchange goes under, you don't lose your bitcoin. However, the responsibilities of holding your own bitcoin are significant.

To hold bitcoin in a custodial service, on the other hand, is to trust a third party to store and secure your bitcoin for you. Almost any service where you can buy bitcoin also offers bitcoin custody services. In fact, when you initially buy bitcoin, it typically resides with the service until you move it off. Using a custodial service means you potentially benefit from people who are experts at holding and securing bitcoin, but you've added to the equation an element of third-party trust.

Owners of gold and other precious metals understand these two options. A holder of gold can buy gold coins or bars and then store them in a safe in his home—that's self-custody. He's responsible to make sure his safe and his house are secure. Or he can pay a company to hold his gold in one of its vaults—that's a custodial service. Here he outsources his security to that company.

Like gold, bitcoin gives users the option to manage their own security. Understanding how security works for both self-custody and for custodial services will help us to know the best option for where to hold our bitcoin. Most security in our current fiat-money system is via custodial services, for it is taken care of (for better or worse) at the bank level. Even then, however, some personal security is involved as well. For example, you protect your credit cards, you don't walk around in a bad neighborhood holding large wads of cash in your hand, and you keep your banking log-in credentials secret. So even though the bank does most of the hard work in protecting your money, you still have some personal security responsibilities with a custodial service.

What, then, are the advantages and disadvantages of self-custody versus a custodial service?

When you self-custody, you have complete and total control over your money; you don't need to trust any third party. Self-custody also gives you total control over whom you send your money to, while a custodial service might restrict whom you can send your bitcoin to or limit how much you can send at any given time. Only when you self-custody can you truly "be your own bank." Only when you self-custody do you truly own your own bitcoin. This is the meaning of the bitcoiner saying, "Not your keys, not your coins"—if you don't control the private keys to your bitcoin, you don't truly own that bitcoin.

Now, if your wallet is lost or broken and you also lose your backup seed phrase, then you've lost your funds ... forever. No one can ever get them back for you. If you have poor security, either on the device that holds your bitcoin private keys or another that accesses that device, you open yourself up to hackers who might be able to steal your bitcoin. If you don't know what you're doing and you hold a sizable quantity of bitcoin, you run the risk of catastrophic failure.

Custodial services allow a bitcoin user to outsource the work of securing his bitcoin. No need to worry about losing your backup seed phrase, no need to be concerned with securing your bitcoin: it's all done for you. You only need to secure your password to the service, just like using a bank.

Using a custodial service, however, also means you've lost one of the primary advantages of bitcoin: direct ownership of your funds. All the benefits of bitcoin when it comes to censorship-resistance and trustless payments are gone. Custodial services are akin to banks—you have to trust they are actually holding the funds they claim to hold. You also have to trust that they won't run off with your bitcoin, that they will let you spend your bitcoin, and that they're secure enough to protect your bitcoin (a company holding thousands of bitcoin is a much larger target than most individuals).

Custodial services are beholden to many of the same laws as banks, which means they also must abide by any government edicts to seize a customer's bitcoin. Using a custodial service means that for convenience's sake you've added a layer of third-party trust that isn't required in bitcoin itself. This might be worth it, though, depending on your risk tolerance, technical knowledge, and personal views.

So should you self-custody or use a custodial service? My general advice has always been that it's okay to save smaller amounts of bitcoin with reputable custodial services, but if you're holding any sizable amount (each person must determine what is a "sizable amount" for himself), then learn how to self-custody and do that. Of course, when you start getting into *really* sizable amounts (millions of dollars' worth), then you might want to reconsider custodial services with very trusted and reputable third parties, since the potential of total loss through user error with self-custody would be so enormous.

CHARACTERISTIC OF A HOLDING METHOD	SELF-CUSTODY	CUSTODIAL SERVICE
Total control over your BTC	✓	
Freedom to send any amount of BTC to any person at any time	✓	
No need to trust a third party who could lose or steal your BTC	✓	
Ease of use in securing BTC		✓
No possible total loss of BTC via lost device or seed phrase		✓

Learning more about how self-custody works will help you make that decision.

HARDWARE WALLETS

The best way to self-custody is to use a **hardware wallet**. This is a special physical device that doesn't directly connect to the internet and securely stores the private keys of your bitcoin.

All transactions must be confirmed on the physical device, which means a hacker can't just access your laptop or smartphone or PC via the internet to grab your bitcoin; he would need physical access to your hardware device as well. Dozens of different hardware wallets exist; some of the most popular ones include Blockstream Jade (blockstream.com), Trezor (trezor.io), Ledger (ledger.com), and Coldcard (coldcard.com).

Always purchase a hardware wallet directly from the company that manufactures it. Buying it from a third party introduces the possibility that a malicious actor injected code into the device to steal the bitcoin you store on it.

Each hardware device works a bit differently, but here are the basics. The device is never itself directly connected to the internet. This prevents hackers from accessing the keys stored on the device remotely. When you want to use the device to send bitcoin, you plug it into your computer via a USB port (some devices connect in different ways) and open the software on the computer that interacts with the device. The hardware wallet is also protected by a PIN that you enter directly on the device. You never directly type any security information into your computer; this protects from hackers who might be tracking your computer's keyboard. And if someone actually steals your device, he needs to know your wallet PIN to access it.[108] Obviously, a hardware wallet should be kept in a secure location where it would be difficult for anyone to steal it in the first place.

But what if the device is misplaced or destroyed? Don't worry, all is not lost. You just need your **seed phrase**. Seed phrases are important, so let's review what they are.

[108] There are other layers available to protect the keys on a device even if the wallet is stolen, but that's a more advanced topic.

Seed phrases allow people to have a backup in case of damage to their hardware wallet, which is vital if your device is storing a good amount of bitcoin. A seed phrase is a series of random words—usually twelve, twenty, or twenty-four words—that serve as a backup to the wallet. Believe it or not, this series of words, when input in the correct order on another hardware wallet, is able to restore your original wallet onto that second device. The seed phrase should always be stored offline—typically on a piece of paper or a metal device on which the words are engraved—to protect it from hackers. Never store a seed phrase digitally! *Anyone with access to your seed phrase has complete access to your funds,* so it's vital to physically protect it from theft, not to mention fire and other potential hazards.

Recently, "hybrid devices" also became available. These combine some of the features of self-custody with certain conveniences of a custodial service. Like self-custodial hardware wallets, hybrid devices use a hardware device that gives you complete access to your bitcoin. They are also devised so that bitcoin cannot be sent without your permission. However, unlike a full self-custody device, you store a backup key with the service provider instead of using a seed phrase. If you lose your device, the provider can reestablish access to your funds for you. In this case, your BTC is more truly "yours" than if it were at a custodial service, but you are not completely responsible for maintaining a backup.

However, if you use a hybrid device, you're trusting that the service provider will stay in business—if it shuts down, it can no longer provide backup services. Nevertheless, this option may be a good compromise for beginners, as it keeps the

BTC secure but transfers the responsibility for backups to a third party. And many hybrid devices are more user-friendly than full self-custody hardware wallets. Bitkey (bitkey.world) is the main entry in this space, as of this writing.

Sending and Receiving Bitcoin

Sending bitcoin, especially for the first time, is the most nerve-racking part of the bitcoin process; hopefully one day it will become much more user-friendly.

Whether you are sending bitcoin from a custodial service or from a hardware device, the basic process is the same. The first thing you need to know is the bitcoin address to which you want to send your bitcoin. A bitcoin address will look something like this:

bc1q0mrag879fuk8fdtvv3rt2cek4h35qtyaste5kn

Not exactly easy to remember, is it? Because of this, most bitcoin services include a QR code to copy the address, or, at the very least, a copy button.

Here's your procedure:

- Copy the address.
- Find and select the send button in your wallet.
- Paste the BTC address you copied.
- Enter the amount of BTC to send.
- Confirm your send.

What if you enter the wrong address? If it's an invalid address—one that can't exist on the bitcoin network—most wallets will reject the transaction. But if it is a valid (but wrong) address, then the funds will be sent there and you can never get them back. Always triple-check the address before sending!

Once the BTC has been sent, you wait. Because blocks are created approximately every ten minutes, you typically won't have to wait longer than that for confirmation, but remember that this is an average. Sometimes the interval between blocks can be as long as twenty minutes or more, and sometimes it's less than two minutes. Most wallets will "see" the transaction even before the next block is recorded, since bitcoin nodes are checking every transaction before miners add it to a block. Your wallet will show the transaction as "pending." Once the block with the transaction is confirmed (some wallets wait for multiple confirmations, meaning multiple blocks approved), then it will show as "sent" in your wallet. Congratulations! You are now directly participating in the most moral money system ever created!

Every bitcoin transaction automatically generates a transaction fee, paid for by the sender.[109] This is the opposite of our typical experience, in which the *receiver* of a credit card transaction (the merchant) pays for any transaction fees, although that cost is passed on to the consumer via higher prices. Also unlike credit card transactions, the fee is *not* based on the amount of money being sent. A bitcoin transaction worth one billion dollars might have a transaction fee less than eight dollars, while a transaction worth

---

[109] Many exchanges and other custodial services also add an additional fee paid to them for their services.

eight dollars might also require an eight-dollar fee.[110] The amount of the fee varies constantly. It's based primarily on the amount of traffic on the bitcoin network at the time of sending—more traffic means higher fees.[111] The transaction fee goes to the miner who mines that block, along with the new BTC created in that block. Typically the fees are relatively small—often less than ten dollars—but in very high traffic times they can become quite hefty.

Alongside the tremendous rise in the price of bitcoin has come the similarly tremendous rise in scams associated with bitcoin. Sadly, it's not uncommon to hear of people being swindled out of their bitcoin by manipulative scam artists. And with bitcoin transactions being irreversible, it's usually impossible to recover the funds, even if by some small chance the thief is identified. Be scam-proof:

- Never send bitcoin to anyone without confirming the address.

[110] Early on in bitcoin's history, many bitcoiners dreamed of a world where you could buy a cup of coffee at the local shop using bitcoin directly. While this is technically possible, it's impractical on any real-world scale. The number of transactions per minute in bitcoin is far too small to handle billions of small transactions, and because of that limited block space, the fees for the transactions would be prohibitive. Imagine a fifty-dollar fee for a five-dollar cup of coffee! This is why companies are developing "layer 2" solutions that sit on top of bitcoin and allow for more and cheaper transactions. In those uses, bitcoin is the "base layer," where financial transactions are settled.

[111] Transaction fees are technically based on the size in bytes of the transaction, and they are determined by how little miners are willing to accept to include the transaction in a new block. When traffic is very high, naturally fees rise in the competition to include transactions in the next block, and when traffic is lower, fees decline.

✥ Always treat the security of your hardware device as you would your own physical wallet that carries your cash (or like a safe in your home that holds gold).

✥ Never, ever, ever give out your seed phrase to anyone.

✥ Ignore anyone randomly contacting you by phone or email to request you send them bitcoin. That's always a scam.

As you might imagine, receiving bitcoin is a lot simpler. You must first generate a bitcoin address from your wallet. Remember that each bitcoin wallet controls many addresses, and it doesn't matter which one you use. Typically a wallet will have a "receive" option, and when you select that option you are given one of the addresses under the control of your wallet (it might generate a QR code as well, to allow smartphones to capture the address more easily). Give this address to the person sending you bitcoin, and wait for your wallet to show the transaction. As with sending bitcoin, you might first see that the wallet indicates a transaction is pending. Once the transaction is confirmed on the blockchain, it will be marked as received in your wallet, and your wallet will show your new balance.

"Hodling" Bitcoin

Once you own bitcoin, what do you do with it? Well, you hold on to it—or as bitcoiners say, you **hodl**.[112] Because bitcoin is a hard asset, it's more likely to go up in value over the long

---

[112] This is not a typo. In the bitcoin world, to hold bitcoin is called "hodling," after a famous forum post from 2013 in which an inebriated bitcoin user misspelled the word "hold" when asserting that he would not sell even though the price was dropping.

term (four-plus years) in comparison to fiat money, although it may rise and fall in the short term. This is what has happened consistently in bitcoin's first sixteen years. It's a better money than fiat money, so most people tend to spend bitcoin more rarely than they do fiat money. It bears out Gresham's Law. If you know that the value of your money will increase in the future, you are more likely to hesitate before spending it, especially on frivolous items. As a hard asset, bitcoin is made to save, or hodl, as the case may be.

Bitcoin can be used for buying and selling goods, and many merchants accept bitcoin. But until bitcoin gets past the volatile store-of-value establishment phase, its use as a medium of exchange (to say nothing of its use as a unit of account) is limited. In extreme situations, such as in a hyperinflating economy or under an oppressive government, bitcoin can be a literal lifesaver, but for those in relatively stable economies, the best use case for bitcoin is simply to hodl it.

This is not always easy. What if you buy a significant amount of bitcoin in June only to see the value in fiat terms drop 50 percent by August? It's happened before. But bitcoin has also always grown in value over time. Pick any date after January 3, 2009, and look up the price of BTC on that date. Now look four years later—the price of BTC will be up, likely quite a bit. But if you selected a day one month, five months, or a year after that initial date, it's not unlikely that the price was down. As they say in investment circles, past performance is no guarantee of future returns, but based on what we know about bitcoin versus fiat money, my money's on bitcoin in the future.

Conclusion

Will Bitcoin Become the World's Money?

*I don't believe that we shall ever
have a good money again before we
take the thing out of the hands of
government — that is, we can't take them
violently out of the hands of government;
all we can do is by some sly, roundabout
way introduce something they can't stop.*

—Friedrich A. Hayek[113]

[113] Friedrich A. Hayek, "An Interview with F. A. Hayek," interview by James U. Blanchard III, University of Freiburg, Germany, May 1, 1984, posted April 8, 2018, YouTube, https://www.youtube.com/watch?v=s-k_Fc63tZI.

THE FIAT MONETARY system we all live under is immoral. It steals our purchasing power over time; it empowers our rulers to wage unjust wars; it favors the rich over the poor; it fosters financial nihilism among our young. Obviously we should oppose this system, yet most of us have little or no power to change it. What is our responsibility as those who live under it?

First, we should consider our personal responsibility. Am I saying that we all need to exchange our dollars for bitcoin and refuse to do business in any other form of money? No; that's simply impossible to do while upholding our responsibilities to care for others and ourselves. We will all continue to use fiat money for the foreseeable future. Yet we need to consider the root of some of the world's financial and political problems and work to correct them.

In the 1980s, Pope John Paul II wrote about "structures of sin." By this he meant sinful patterns and ideas that permeate the culture around us and from which we cannot escape. These structures of sin are "rooted in personal sin, and thus always linked to the concrete acts of individuals who introduce these structures, consolidate them and make them difficult to remove."[114]

[114] Pope John Paul II, Encyclical Letter *Sollicitudo Rei Socialis* (December 30, 1987), no. 36, https://www.vatican.va/content/john-paul-ii/en/encyclicals/documents/hf_jp-ii_enc_30121987_sollicitudo-rei-socialis.html.

One example of a modern "structure of sin" is the culture of death, particularly the abortion industry. Without wanting to, even the most ardent pro-life person supports this industry in various ways, whether it be by buying products from companies that donate to Planned Parenthood or just from paying taxes to a government that funds Planned Parenthood. We can't escape it, and while we might not be personally responsible for the evils committed in this culture of death, we do sadly participate in it to varying degrees. That's the insidious evil of structures of sin. Yet we can each individually make an effort to combat the culture of death, whether it be by prayer, or helping a woman in a crisis pregnancy, or through political action. Doing nothing is not an option when such an oppressive evil is at work among us.

The immoral fiat monetary system, dominated by the U.S. dollar, is another modern structure of sin. Powerful individuals introduced this system to further empower and enrich themselves, and over time the fiat system has permeated our society, making it incredibly difficult to remove. It fosters and encourages personal sins all around us. We cannot help being part of it, but we should work to fix it. People of faith historically have been at the forefront of fighting systemic injustice, from racism to abortion. We need also to resist the systemic injustice of the fiat monetary system.

Yet what can we do? All the great powers of the world (backed by all their militaries) support fiat because it keeps them in power. No violent revolution will take down that system. But all is not hopeless: bitcoin offers an alternative, one that might over time peacefully replace fiat, and one in which we can all participate. As quoted at the beginning of this chapter, economist Friedrich A. Hayek, winner of the 1974 Nobel Prize in economics, actually predicted this possibility more than forty years ago when he said that immoral fiat money can't be replaced by violence, but only by introducing an alternative in a "sly, roundabout way" that governments can't stop.

Forcing a new monetary system on the world would be ugly and it would be bloody, and in the end might very well not succeed. But Satoshi Nakamoto simply created one and offered it to the world for free. Couldn't this be the "sly, roundabout way" to undermine and eventually replace fiat money? We can all be on the forefront of making this happen in ways large and small: by advocating for our political leaders to allow bitcoin to flourish; by encouraging others to use bitcoin; or just by putting some of our own savings into bitcoin.

The world will be better off on a bitcoin standard than a fiat standard.[115] Bitcoin is more efficient than a fiat-money system, but more importantly, it is far more moral. With a fixed monetary supply grounded in mathematics, bitcoin avoids the devaluing over time that comes about due to the inevitable inflation of a money supply controlled by fallen man. This doesn't mean bitcoin's price will always have exponential rises in the future—and that's good. It does mean that bitcoin will be a way for the average person to keep from falling behind without engaging in risky investments. It will be a return to the days of savings actually being savings and, we can hope, the end of financial nihilism.

---

[115] See the work of Saifedean Ammous, author of perhaps the best book written on bitcoin, *The Bitcoin Standard* (Wiley, 2018) and also of a companion book, *The Fiat Standard* (The Saif House, 2021).

Widespread adoption of bitcoin will signal a return to a savings mentality and a turning away from consumerism. With money retaining its value over time, people will think more long-term. Instead of pursuing the immediate but fleeting gratification that comes with buying things of little value, those living under a bitcoin standard will naturally be incentivized to save for their future and for their children, something everyone should support. In a bitcoin economy religious people would also be less vulnerable to being financially canceled. And, government leaders would be hamstrung in their efforts to lead us into unjust and endless wars.

Will a society under a bitcoin standard be a utopia? Of course not. When Thomas More coined the word in his classic work *Utopia*, he knew the underlying Greek meant "no place." Here on earth, no place can be a utopia. The effects of Original Sin afflict us all. People will still steal and lie and commit other crimes in a bitcoin-standard world, just as now, but the ability of powerful governments and institutions to systematically commit those crimes will be lessened, and the incentives built into the monetary system will favor virtue far more than those of the fiat system do.

Bitcoin is not a perfect form of money. Perfection in our money is impossible on this side of Heaven, and Heaven doesn't need any form of money, so it doesn't exist there, either. But it's a more moral form of money; in fact, the most moral form ever used by man. While bitcoin will not solve all our problems, it can and should topple the structure of sin that is the fiat monetary system.

Selected Bibliography

BELOW ARE A few books that can help one further understand bitcoin, particularly as a new form of money.

Alden, Lyn. *Broken Money: Why Our Financial System Is Failing Us and How We Can Make It Better.* Timestamp Press, 2023.

Ammous, Saifedean. *The Bitcoin Standard: The Decentralized Alternative to Central Banking.* Wiley, 2018.

Antonopoulos, Andreas M. *Mastering Bitcoin: Unlocking Digital Cryptocurrencies.* O'Reilly Media, 2014.

Bailey, Andrew M., Bradley Rettler, and Craig Warmke. *Resistance Money: A Philosophical Case for Bitcoin.* Taylor & Francis, 2024.

Bhatia, Nik. *Layered Money: From Gold and Dollars to Bitcoin and Central Bank Digital Currencies.* Published by the author, 2021.

Champagne, Phil. *The Book of Satoshi: The Collected Writings of Bitcoin Creator Satoshi Nakamoto.* E53 Publishing, 2014.

Lewis, Parker A. *Gradually, Then Suddenly: A Framework for Understanding Bitcoin as Money.* Gradually Then Suddenly, 2023.

Yakes, Eric. *The 7th Property: Bitcoin and the Monetary Revolution.* Black Poodle Publishing, 2021.

Acknowledgments

WHEN I STUDIED systems analysis and economics in college and later theology in a master's program, I never imagined my varied education could all be brought together in one book. Yet here we are. In addition to my professors, numerous others helped me understand money, morality, and bitcoin, how they all come together, and how to share this powerful knowledge with others.

⁜ I'm grateful for my wife, Suzan, who has not only tolerated but sincerely supported my obsession with this magic internet money for more than a decade. She was the one who pushed me to write this book, and she's also the wonderful editor who helped it come together.

⁜ My dad first taught me the value of money. His frugality and responsible saving have been a model for me throughout my life. I'll always be thankful for him.

⁜ I first became engaged with bitcoin after hearing a podcast with Thomas E. Woods and Erik Vorhees in 2013. It's likely I would have eventually embraced bitcoin without this experience, but they lit the initial fire.

⁜ The work of Andreas Antonopoulos in the early years of bitcoin helped countless people, including myself, to better understand how bitcoin works and its value proposition.

✣ I'm indebted to Saifedean Ammous for writing *The Bitcoin Standard*. Even though I'd already been involved with the bitcoin community for five years when the book was published, Ammous's work crystallized for me what made bitcoin unique among cryptocurrencies.

✣ The tireless efforts of the "Bitcoin OGs" — Hal Finney, Roger Ver, Charlie Shrem, Ross Ulbricht, the Winklevoss twins, Erik Vorhees, Gavin Andresen, and others — cannot be forgotten. Without them, bitcoin would never have gotten off the ground.

✣ And of course, I'm thankful for Satoshi Nakamoto, whoever and wherever he may be. He left the world with a means to make it a better place to live, without expecting any reward for himself. Wherever he is, I say thank you!

Glossary

address, bitcoin: A publicly available string of alphanumeric characters that serves as a destination for bitcoin transactions. It is connected cryptographically to a bitcoin **private key** such that only a possessor of the private key can access the bitcoin held by the public address.

anarchist: A person who opposes governments and laws that are not part of a voluntary association.

barter: *See* **direct exchange**.

bitcoin: A cryptocurrency that allows a person to hold and transfer value over the Internet in a trustless manner. It ranks high in the seven **monetary properties**, making it an ideal form of money.

bitcoin white paper: A 2008 document by the pseudonymous author Satoshi Nakamoto that introduced bitcoin as a new "peer-to-peer electronic cash system."

block, bitcoin: A group of **bitcoin transactions** that is added to the **bitcoin blockchain** by a **bitcoin miner**. Once a block is added to the blockchain, all transactions included in that block are considered confirmed.

blockchain: A digital public ledger of all bitcoin transactions. Transactions are grouped together in a **block** and then added to a "chain" of previous blocks of transactions.

block reward: The amount of bitcoin distributed to the **bitcoin miner** who confirms a new **block** on the bitcoin **blockchain**. It consists of newly created bitcoin plus any transaction fees.

Cantillon Effect: The phenomenon of unequal distribution of any new money in an economy, first recognized by eighteenth-century French economist Richard Cantillon. Those who are closest to the money benefit the most.

central bank: An institution that manages a country's currency, money supply, and interest rates.

central bank digital currency (CBDC): A **digital money** that uses **blockchain** technology like bitcoin's but gives one entity, usually a country's central bank, total control of the money.

centralization: An organizational system in which one person, or a small group of people, has control over the system. Centralized systems can be efficient, but they are easily corrupted due to the small number of people in control.

confirmation, bitcoin: The process by which a **bitcoin transaction** is verified and added to the bitcoin **blockchain** through the process of **mining**.

consumerism: An economic order that encourages the purchase and consumption of goods and services.

Consumer Price Index (CPI): A system of tracking **price inflation** in the United States in which the price of a "basket" of goods that the average American purchases is tracked over time. Although CPI measures are used to designate price inflation, those who manage it can change the goods in the CPI basket. This has resulted in a lower reported level of price inflation than what is actually occurring in the economy.

cryptocurrency: A digital form of currency that uses cryptography for security and resides solely on the internet. The first cryptocurrency was bitcoin.

custodial service: A means of holding bitcoin in which a third party secures the bitcoin for a customer and has ultimate control of it.

debanked: Describes a person or organization that has lost the ability to use banking services, typically due to an order or pressure from the government. Most often, it refers to losing banking services in spite of having broken no laws.

debt: An amount of money borrowed by one party from another with the obligation to repay the amount, usually with interest or other finance charges as well.

decentralization: An organizational system in which no one person, or small group of people, has control over the system. Decentralized systems are difficult to corrupt, since power is distributed among many members.

difficulty adjustment: Part of the bitcoin **protocol** in which the solution to the mathematical challenge needed to mine bitcoin is changed in order to keep the average time interval between creation of new **blocks** at ten minutes.

digital money: Money that can be held and transferred through the internet. A digital money can either represent another form of money (as in the case of digital **fiat money**), or it can be the form of money itself (as in the case of bitcoin).

direct exchange: A trade between people in which goods and services are exchanged directly, as opposed to a trade using money in an intermediary transaction (**indirect exchange**).

divisibility: A monetary property that describes the extent to which a form of money can be subdivided into various amounts that are suitable for purchases of different sizes.

double-spend problem: Being able to spend the same units of **digital money** multiple times by copying that digital money, thus making the money worthless.

durability: A monetary property that describes the extent to which a form of money does not rot or rust or break easily, so that it can be saved over time without concern for its fragility.

Ethereum: A **cryptocurrency** launched in 2015 that promised to be the "world's computer" through the use of smart contracts.

exchange, bitcoin: A company that facilitates the buying and selling of bitcoin. It typically also acts as a **custodial service** for holding bitcoin.

Federal Reserve System: The **central bank** of the United States, charged with managing the monetary policy of the country through a variety of means, including the printing of new **fiat money**.

fiat money: A form of money created by a government and backed only by trust in that government. The Latin word *fiat* means "let it be done," and the term *fiat money* refers to the government declaration "Let this money be done [created]."

fractional reserve banking: A system by which a bank holds only a fraction of its deposits. The rest of the money is used to offer loans and other financial services to other customers.

fungibility: A monetary property that describes the extent to which individual units of a form of money are similar such that one unit is just as acceptable as another.

gold-paper monetary system: *See* **gold standard**.

gold standard: A monetary system in which gold is the base money, but other forms of money, such as paper and **digital money**, are used in most exchanges. Under a gold standard, all forms of money used can, by law, be exchanged for gold.

Greater Fool Theory: A theory that states that the way to make money through **investment** is to find someone to buy a worthless good the investor holds at a higher price than the investor paid.

halving, bitcoin: An automated system in the bitcoin protocol by which the **block reward** is cut in half. It occurs every 210,000 **blocks**, which is approximately every four years.

hard asset: A good that keeps its value over time, even in the face of inflation. Examples include real estate and precious metals.

hard fork: A software upgrade in which past versions of the software are incompatible with versions after the upgrade.

hard money: *See* **sound money.**

hardware wallet: A physical device, typically not directly connected to the internet, that controls the private keys for **bitcoin addresses**.

hodl: A term for saving, or holding, bitcoin. In 2013, an inebriated bitcoin user on a bitcoin internet form misspelled the word *hold* when asserting that he would not sell even though the price was dropping.

independence: A monetary property that describes the extent to which a form of money cannot be controlled by any one person or entity (such as a government or a corporation).

indirect exchange: A trade that occurs when at least one person accepts an item that he does not intend to use directly but, instead, plans to trade away in the future to get something else. The most common good used in indirect exchange is money.

inflation: An increase in the **monetary supply**, usually through producing more money by some natural means (such as gold mining) or by creating new money via government action in a **fiat money** system. Also referred to as monetary inflation.

intrinsic value: The belief that an object has value that is outside of anyone's subjective perspective. In reality, a good's value is based on what people are willing to pay for it.

investment: Money set aside (**savings**) that is spent in order to increase future income.

investment risk: The probability that an investment's actual returns will differ from the expected returns, potentially leading to a loss of some or all of the investment.

leverage, financial: The use of borrowed capital (**debt**) to increase the potential return on investment. It typically involves using debt to finance assets or operations in hopes that the income or capital gains from the investment will exceed the cost of borrowing.

libertarian: a person who advocates for liberty, emphasizing individual freedom, voluntary association, and minimal government intervention in both personal and economic matters.

medium of exchange: A good that is obtained not to be consumed or in the production of another good but primarily in exchange for other goods. One of the three purposes of money, along with **store of value** and **unit of account**.

memecoin: A type of **cryptocurrency** inspired by an internet meme, character, or trend. Many memecoins are a way to represent an enthusiastic online community and do not support any underlying technology project.

miner, bitcoin: A computer on the bitcoin network that secures the network and adds new **blocks** to the **blockchain**. This is achieved by means of a competition between miners to solve mathematical challenges, with the winner confirming the latest block of **transactions**. For this win, they are rewarded with bitcoin (*see* **block reward**).

monetary inflation: see **inflation**.

monetary properties: Seven properties that indicate whether a good is able to serve as a useful and moral form of money. They include **divisibility, portability, durability, fungibility, verifiability, scarcity**, and **independence**.

monetary supply: The total amount of money in an economy.

natural law: A philosophical concept that recognizes the existence of a set of inherent principles, derived from nature and reason, that govern human conduct.

network effect: The economic principle that the value of a product or service increases as more people use it.

node, bitcoin: A computer that runs the core bitcoin software and stores the entire bitcoin **blockchain**. Nodes validate **bitcoin transactions,** and each node checks with every other node to confirm the validity of their copy and every other copy.

open-source software: Software code that is viewable by the public. This gives the software greater security, since any bugs or security holes can be found more quickly.

portability: A monetary property that describes the extent to which a form of money is easy to move across distances, which means it must hold a lot of value in a small package.

price discovery: The determination of the price of a good through the interactions of buyers and sellers.

price inflation: An increase in prices over a period of time. Often referred to simply as "inflation," it is actually the consequence of monetary **inflation**, as more money in an economy leads to higher prices in that economy.

private key: A large, randomly generated number that allows a user to access bitcoin held by the corresponding **bitcoin addresses** controlled by that key. **Bitcoin wallets** store private keys and so allow users to access their bitcoin.

proof of stake: A **cryptocurrency** system that generates new units of a cryptocurrency and validates new transactions by requiring participants to lock up a certain amount of their cryptocurrency as a stake.

proof of work: A **cryptocurrency** system that generates new units of a cryptocurrency and confirms new transactions by requiring participants (**miners**) to expend computational effort to solve a difficult mathematical puzzle. This is the system used by bitcoin.

protocol, Internet: A set of rules that determines how a particular piece of software operates on the Internet.

pseudonymous: The use of another name or identification instead of one's real name. All **bitcoin transactions** are pseudonymous, in that public **bitcoin addresses** are used instead of names. Note that connections can be made at times using various analysis tools; this differentiates this system from anonymous ones, in which there is no revealed connection between the name or address being used and the real name.

public-key cryptography: A cryptographic system that uses pairs of keys that are mathematically linked to each other: a public key, which can be widely distributed, and a **private key**, which is kept secret.

purchasing power: The value of money in terms of the amount of goods or services that one unit of money can buy.

savings: An amount of money set aside when income is greater than spending.

satoshi (sat): The smallest denomination of bitcoin. It is equal to 0.00000001 BTC.

scarcity: A monetary property that describes the extent to which the supply of a form of money is difficult to increase.

seed phrase: A random set of typically twelve, twenty, or twenty-four words that acts as a backup for someone's **bitcoin wallet**. It can be used to create a new instance of that wallet on another device.

self-custody: A means of holding bitcoin that is completely under a user's control.

smart contract: A way to simulate real-world contracts programmatically, typically on a **blockchain**.

soft fork: A software upgrade in which past versions of the software are compatible with versions after the upgrade.

sound money: A form of money that is stable and reliable and possesses qualities such as scarcity and fungibility that make it an effective **store of value, medium of exchange**, and **unit of account**. The term *sound money* originated from one of the historic phenomena of government monetary fraud. To enrich themselves, certain governments sneaked other metals into gold or silver coins. These adulterated coins sounded different from authentic ones when dropped onto a hard surface, so citizens eventually realized that they could determine whether a coin was legitimate by the sound it made when dropped.

stablecoin: A type of **cryptocurrency** whose value is pegged to a fiat money such as the U.S. dollar. Stablecoins are typically controlled by a centralized organization that, in order to maintain the peg, holds cash and cash equivalents that match the total amount of the stablecoin supply.

stable currency: A form of money whose value does not significantly change over time in terms of purchasing power.

store of value: A good that is considered valuable and holds that value over time; one of the three purposes of money, along with **medium of exchange** and **unit of account**.

subsidiarity: the principle by which decisions and responsibilities should be handled at the lowest, most local level of authority capable of addressing them effectively, with higher levels intervening only when necessary.

temperance: "The moral virtue that moderates the attraction of pleasures and provides balance in the use of created goods" (*CCC* 1809).

time preference: The degree to which a person will delay gratification in order to receive a greater benefit down the road. Low time preference means willingness to forgo instant gratification in order to receive something greater at a future time. High time preference means preferring a good right now over a greater good later.

transaction, bitcoin: The operation in which bitcoin under the control of one **bitcoin address** is sent to another address. A transaction must be confirmed before it becomes permanent on the bitcoin **blockchain**.

unbanked: Describes a person who has no bank account and is unable to obtain one due to poverty or a broken or corrupt banking system.

unit of account: The ability of a money to be used for pricing goods and services; one of the three purposes of money, along with a **store of value** and **medium of exchange**.

verifiability: A monetary property that describes the extent to which a seller of goods or services is able to check that the form of money he is paid is what it appears to be. If counterfeiting is difficult to accomplish or easy to spot, a money has high verifiability.

wallet, bitcoin: Software that controls a set of **private keys** and public **bitcoin addresses** in order to allow a user to hold, send, and receive bitcoin. A bitcoin wallet can be an app on a phone, a program on a desktop or laptop computer, a web application, or a specialized hardware device.

About the Author

ERIC SAMMONS IS the editor in chief of *Crisis Magazine*. He holds a degree in systems analysis with a concentration in economics from Miami University in Ohio, as well as a master's degree in theology from Franciscan University of Steubenville. Sammons is the author of several books, including *Who Do You Say I Am?: Unlocking the 24 Titles Given to Jesus in the Gospel of Matthew* (Sophia Institute Press) and *Bitcoin Basics: 101 Questions and Answers* (Saragossa Press).

Sammons worked for more than fifteen years in the software development field, including ten years leading his own software firm. He also spent five years as director of evangelization for the Diocese of Venice in Florida.

Sophia Institute

SOPHIA INSTITUTE IS a nonprofit institution that seeks to nurture the spiritual, moral, and cultural life of souls and to spread the gospel of Christ in conformity with the authentic teachings of the Roman Catholic Church.

Sophia Institute Press fulfills this mission by offering translations, reprints, and new publications that afford readers a rich source of the enduring wisdom of mankind.

Sophia Institute also operates the popular online resource CatholicExchange.com. *Catholic Exchange* provides world news from a Catholic perspective as well as daily devotionals and articles that will help readers to grow in holiness and live a life consistent with the teachings of the Church.

In 2013, Sophia Institute launched Sophia Institute for Teachers to renew and rebuild Catholic culture through service to Catholic education. With the goal of nurturing the spiritual, moral, and cultural life of souls, and an abiding respect for the role and work of teachers, we strive to provide materials and programs that are at once enlightening to the mind and ennobling to the heart; faithful and complete, as well as useful and practical.

Sophia Institute gratefully recognizes the Solidarity Association for preserving and encouraging the growth of our apostolate over the course of many years. Without their generous and timely support, this book would not be in your hands.

www.SophiaInstitute.com
www.CatholicExchange.com
www.SophiaTeachers.org

Sophia Institute Press is a registered trademark of Sophia Institute.
Sophia Institute is a tax-exempt institution as defined by the
Internal Revenue Code, Section 501(c)(3). Tax ID 22-2548708.